D0568942

KF4750 .C493 2006

Civil liberties

DATE DUE

DEMCO, INC. 38-2931

Colorado Mountain College
Quigley Library
3000 County Road 114
Glenwood Springs, CO 81601

INTRODUCING
ISSUES
WITH

OPPOSING VIEWPOINTS®

CIVIL LIBERTIES

Other books in the Introducing Issues
with Opposing Viewpoints series:

AIDS
Alcohol
Cloning
The Death Penalty
Gangs
Gay Marriage
Genetic Engineering
Smoking
Terrorism

INTRODUCING ISSUES WITH

OPPOSING VIEWPOINTS®

CIVIL LIBERTIES

Andrea C. Nakaya, *Book Editor*

Bruce Glassman, *Vice President*
Bonnie Szumski, *Publisher, Series Editor*
Helen Cothran, *Managing Editor*

OPPOSING VIEWPOINTS® SERIES

GREENHAVEN PRESS
An imprint of Thomson Gale, a part of The Thomson Corporation

THOMSON
GALE

Detroit • New York • San Francisco • San Diego • New Haven, Conn. • Waterville, Maine • London • Munich

© 2006 Thomson Gale, a part of The Thomson Corporation.

Thomson and Star Logo are trademarks and Gale and Greenhaven Press are registered trademarks used herein under license.

For more information, contact
Greenhaven Press
27500 Drake Rd.
Farmington Hills, MI 48331-3535
Or you can visit our Internet site at http://www.gale.com

ALL RIGHTS RESERVED.
No part of this work covered by the copyright hereon may be reproduced or used in any form or by any means—graphic, electronic, or mechanical, including photocopying, recording, tap-ing, Web distribution or information storage retrieval systems—without the written permission of the publisher.

Every effort has been made to trace the owners of copyrighted material.

LIBRARY OF CONGRESS CATALOGING-IN-PUBLICATION DATA

Civil liberties / Andrea C. Nakaya, book editor.
    p. cm. — (Introducing issues with opposing viewpoints)
Includes bibliographical references and index.
ISBN 0-7377-3387-X (lib. : alk. paper)
1. Civil rights—United States—Popular works. 2. Terrorism—United States—Prevention—Popular works. I. Nakaya, Andrea C., 1976– . II. Series.
KF4750.C493 2006
342.7308'5—dc22

2005046144

Printed in the United States of America

CONTENTS

Chapter 3: Are Civil Liberties in the United States Threatened?

Indulging in a wide spectrum of ideas, beliefs, and perspectives is a critical cornerstone of democracy. After all, it is often debates over differences of opinion, such as whether to legalize abortion, how to treat prisoners, or when to enact the death penalty that shape our society and drive it forward. Such diversity of thought is frequently regarded as the hallmark of a healthy and civilized culture. As the Reverend Clifford Schutjer of the First Congregational Church in Mansfield, Ohio, declared in a 2001 sermon, "Surrounding oneself with only like-minded people, restricting what we listen to or read only to what we find agreeable is irresponsible. Refusing to entertain doubts once we make up our minds is a subtle but deadly form of arrogance." With this advice in mind, Introducing Issues with Opposing Viewpoints books aim to open readers' minds to the critically divergent views that comprise our world's most important debates.

Introducing Issues with Opposing Viewpoints simplifies for students the enormous and often overwhelming mass of material now available via print and electronic media. Collected in every volume is an array of opinions that capture the essence of a particular controversy or topic. Introducing Issues with Opposing Viewpoints books embody the spirit of nineteenth-century journalist Charles A. Dana's axiom: "Fight for your opinions, but do not believe that they contain the whole truth, or the only truth." Absorbing such contrasting opinions teaches students to analyze the strength of an argument and compare it to its opposition. From this process readers can inform and strengthen their own opinions, or be exposed to new information that will change their minds. Introducing Issues with Opposing Viewpoints is a mosaic of different voices. The authors are statesmen, pundits, academics, journalists, corporations, and ordinary people who have felt compelled to share their experiences and ideas in a public forum. Their words have been collected from newspapers, journals, books, speeches, interviews, and the Internet, the fastest growing body of opinionated material in the world.

Introducing Issues with Opposing Viewpoints shares many of the well-known features of its critically acclaimed parent series, Opposing Viewpoints. The articles are presented in a pro/con format, allowing readers to absorb divergent perspectives side by side. Active reading questions preface each viewpoint, requiring the student to approach the material thoughtfully and carefully. Useful charts, graphs, and cartoons supplement each article. A thorough introduction provides readers with crucial background on an issue. An annotated bibliography points the reader toward articles, books, and Web sites that contain additional information on the topic. An appendix of organizations to contact contains a wide variety of charities, nonprofit organizations, political groups, and private enterprises that each hold a position on the issue at hand. Finally, a comprehensive index allows readers to locate content quickly and efficiently.

Introducing Issues with Opposing Viewpoints is also significantly different from Opposing Viewpoints. As the series title implies, its presentation will help introduce students to the concept of opposing viewpoints, and learn to use this material to aid in critical writing and debate. The series' four-color, accessible format makes the books attractive and inviting to readers of all levels. In addition, each viewpoint has been carefully edited to maximize a reader's understanding of the content. Short but thorough viewpoints capture the essence of an argument. A substantial, thought-provoking essay question placed at the end of each viewpoint asks the student to further investigate the issues raised in the viewpoint, compare and contrast two authors' arguments, or consider how one might go about forming an opinion on the topic at hand. Each viewpoint contains sidebars that include at-a-glance information and handy statistics. A Facts About section located in the back of the book further supplies students with relevant facts and figures.

Following in the tradition of the Opposing Viewpoints series, Greenhaven Press continues to provide readers with invaluable exposure to the controversial issues that shape our world. As John Stuart Mill once wrote: "The only way in which a human being can make some approach to knowing the whole of a subject is by hearing what can be said about it by persons of every variety of opinion and studying all modes in which it can be looked at by every character of mind. No wise man ever acquired his wisdom in any mode but this." It is to this principle that Introducing Issues with Opposing Viewpoints books are dedicated.

INTRODUCTION

"In any civilized society the most important task is achieving a proper balance between freedom and order."

— U.S. Supreme Court justice William H. Rehnquist

The Fifth Amendment to the U.S. Constitution states, "No person shall be . . . deprived of life, liberty, or property, without due process of law." Following the September 11, 2001, terrorist attacks and America's initiation of a war on terrorism, however, hundreds of people have been deprived of liberty by the federal government, without such due process. U.S. citizen José Padilla is one of them. Padilla was arrested in May 2002 on suspicion of conspiring to build and detonate a dirty bomb (a conventional bomb laced with radioactive material). He was imprisoned without access to a lawyer and no charges were filed against him. As of this writing he is still being held by the federal government, without the benefit of due process.

As Padilla's story illustrates, while the Constitution does guarantee numerous civil liberties, the government can take action to restrict these liberties. This often occurs during times of war or other extreme circumstances, where restrictions are made in an effort to ensure national security. In the war on terrorism, many civil liberties have been restricted, including the denial of due process for suspected terrorists. This has spurred heated debate over when, if ever, the government may curtail civil liberties.

Since September 11 the federal government continues to incarcerate hundreds of suspected terrorists and deny them the right to due process. It argues that such imprisonment allows law enforcement to obtain vital information about potential terrorist attacks. According to Vice President Richard Cheney, "These are bad people. . . . They may well have information about future terrorist attacks against the United States. We need that information." In order to get that information, the government argues, due process must sometimes be temporarily suspended. For example, the government maintains that giving José Padilla

Attorneys for detainees at Guantánamo Bay hold a press conference in 2004. The government maintains that suspected terrorists must sometimes be imprisoned without due process.

access to a lawyer or a trial will ruin attempts to obtain important information from him. "Even seemingly minor interruptions can have profound psychological impacts on the delicate subject-interrogator relationship," it argues, "Only after such time as Padilla has perceived that help is not on the way can the United States reasonably expect to obtain all possible intelligence information."

According to the government, incarceration of suspected terrorists without due process has helped them prevent another tragedy like September 11. For example, in a 2004 Supreme Court case challenging the detention of suspected terrorists at the Guantánamo Bay detention center in Cuba, the government maintained:

> The intelligence gathered at Guantánamo has been vital . . . to efforts to disrupt the al Qaeda terrorist network and prevent additional attacks on the United States and its allies. Among other things, Guantánamo detainees have revealed al Qaeda leadership structures, funding mechanisms, training and selection programs, and potential modes of attack. In addition, detainees have provided a continuous source of information to confirm other intelligence reports concerning unfolding terrorist plots or other developments in the conflict.

Secretary of Defense Donald Rumsfeld further argues that many of the detainees, if free, would be attempting to inflict harm on Americans. "There's no question there are a number down in Guantánamo Bay who, every time anyone walks by, threaten to kill Americans the first chance they get," he says. He believes that keeping these people incarcerated is "just plain common sense."

Civil liberties advocates argue, however, that while some of those imprisoned seem to deserve their fate, hundreds of others do not. As the hunt for terrorists continues, both temporary U.S. residents and citizens have related numerous stories detailing their unfair treatment. The American Civil Liberties Union (ACLU) cites the case of "Mr. H," a Pakistani man who has lived in the United States for eighteen years and is the sole provider for his wife and his four-year-old son, a U.S. citizen. According to the ACLU, Mr. H was arrested in 2001 after a coworker at the hospital where he worked complained that he was "acting suspiciously." Based only on the accusation that Mr. H was wearing his surgical mask more than necessary, he was arrested and detained for six months. Sidina Ould Moustapha, a citizen of Mauritania, was also arrested in 2001, on charges of overstaying his visa. While Moustapha offered to voluntarily leave the country, he was instead imprisoned for five months, without any charges filed against him. During that time he was not allowed to contact his wife and two young children in Mauritania.

In addition to being denied due process, many terrorist suspects charge that while imprisoned, they have been severely abused. For example,

Jamal Udeen, a British Muslim who denies any links to terrorism, spent more than two years in the Guantánamo Bay detention center. During that time, he alleges that he and other prisoners were subject to torture, sexual degradation, forced drugging, and religious persecution. "After a while we stopped asking for human rights," says Udeen of his inhumane treatment there, "We wanted animal rights." Tarek Dergoul, who also claims innocence, was released from Guantánamo in 2003. He details one particularly horrific incident of abuse:

> [The guards] pepper-sprayed me in the face, and I started vomiting. They pinned me down and attacked me, poking their fingers in my eyes, and forced my head into the toilet pan and flushed. They tied me up like a beast and then they were kneeling on me, kicking and punching. Finally they dragged me out of the cell in chains, into the [recreation] yard, and shaved my beard, my hair, my eyebrows.

A protester in Cincinnati demonstrates against restrictions on civil liberties.

As the debate over civil liberties and security continues, many people urge that while short-term imprisonment of suspected terrorists may be justified, the federal government does not have the right to detain people for years without due process. Journalist Richard Cohen explains the belief that national security must be balanced with civil liberties. "I was nearby when the twin towers went down," he says, "Hardly a day goes by that I do not think about it. I fear terrorists. . . . But I also fear a government that takes it upon itself to deprive a citizen—any citizen—of his basic rights." Recent Supreme Court decisions also urge the government to reevaluate its position on civil liberties. In June 2004 the Court stated that while the government does need the power to protect its citizens from terrorism, it must also protect their civil liberties. Justice Sandra Day O'Connor explained, "A state of war is not a blank check for the president when it comes to the rights of the nation's citizens."

Suspension of due process is not the only challenge to civil liberties in America's war on terrorism. There have been many others, including government surveillance, racial profiling, and suppression of dissent. As the debate over civil liberties illustrates, the reality of constitutional guarantees may not be absolute protection of civil liberties, but often involves a balancing act. The authors of *Introducing Issues with Opposing Viewpoints: Civil Liberties* offer various perspectives on this issue as they debate how the civil liberties of the individual can best be balanced with the protection of society.

CHAPTER 1

Should Limits Be Placed on Freedom of Expression?

A protester burns the American flag in protest of government policies.

Flag Desecration Should Be Banned

John Andretti

"Nothing tears down America more than burning the flag."

Throughout U.S. history, there have been numerous unsuccessful attempts to pass a constitutional amendment prohibiting flag burning. In the following viewpoint John Andretti continues the tradition by advocating such an amendment. The flag symbolizes the civil liberties that Americans enjoy, maintains Andretti, and burning it represents a desecration of those liberties. He argues that making flag burning illegal would show respect and loyalty for those liberties and the country. Andretti is a race-car driver for the National Association for Stock Car Auto Racing.

AS YOU READ, CONSIDER THE FOLLOWING QUESTIONS:
1. How was the flag used early in the nation's history, according to the author?
2. According to Andretti, how many Americans want their flag protected?
3. How is the flag used to honor members of the armed forces and veterans of military service, as explained by the author?

John Andretti, testimony before the U.S. Senate Committee on the Judiciary, Washington, DC, March 10, 2004.

By the end of World War II, my father's family had lost everything. He and his brother grew up in a relocation camp in eastern Italy, living there from the time they were eight years old until they were 16. They came to the United States at that point, a land of freedom and opportunity. And I am proud to say they made the most of it.

Sometimes he has a hard time describing it because of the emotion, but my father has told me about seeing that flag of the United States—first when liberated in his native Italy and, later, when "liberated" into a new life for him and his family. The flag of the United States represented goodness and freedom, and that is a lesson he taught to his children—and a lesson I am teaching to my children.

A Symbol of Freedom

Being the father of three it is very important for me to teach my children respect and honor, not only for individuals, but also on a whole, and the flag is a means to that end. Our faith is our foundation, but there must be more, and it must be tangible, and it is found in the flag. . . .

I am very proud to be an American. Military or civilian, native or immigrant, the flag is our bond.

I fly the flag at my home, 24 hours a day. And, yes, it is lighted for all to see. I appreciate what the flag stands for and I know quite well what it means to . . . millions of Americans. . . . I think most of them would be surprised—if not, outraged—to learn that today, in our country, it is legal to physically desecrate the flag of the United States.

Importance of a Symbol

There are those who say the flag is only a symbol, but symbols are important. Just as it was a symbol of freedom to my then eight-year-old father in Italy and, later, a symbol of opportunity to him and his family as he entered this country for the first time, it had a message.

Race officials rely on symbols, on flags, to communicate with drivers during noisy racing action. Even with radios today, flags are still important and functional in racing. And in quite the same way, our nation's banner is important and functional, and still sends a message.

Millions of Americans believe the flag is a symbol of freedom and opportunity that should be treated with the utmost respect.

In NASCAR [National Association for Stock Car Auto Racing] you'll see flags waved a lot. But there is one flag that gets waved by NASCAR fans more than any other. And that would be the red, white and blue of Old Glory.

Early in our nation's history, the flag of the United States was something of a signal flag. Out in front of the troops, it signaled action by our military against the forces that might otherwise overrun us. It serves as a symbol of that very notion today as American troops defend our liberties and protect our interests around the world.

And burning a flag, it seems to me, is a very profound signal that those who desecrate the flag have total disregard for our military. . . .

Americans Want to Protect Their Flag

I once heard a man say that the flag represents the freedom to burn it. I would disagree, and I think most Americans would, too.

The flag is a symbol that represents all that our Nation is and can be. It symbolizes what the people say it symbolizes and the great majority certainly don't believe that includes the freedom to desecrate it.

As a sign to rally for a cause, there can be no greater symbol than our flag. We rally around it in times of crisis, whether a natural dis-

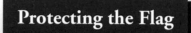

Protecting the Flag

Who would vote for a constitutional amendment to protect the flag?

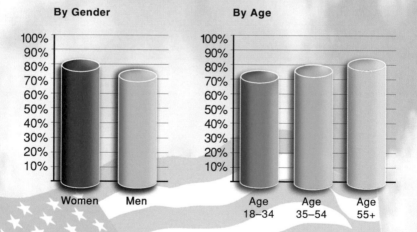

By Gender

100%
90%
80%
70%
60%
50%
40%
30%
20%
10%

Women   Men

By Age

100%
90%
80%
70%
60%
50%
40%
30%
20%
10%

Age 18–34   Age 35–54   Age 55+

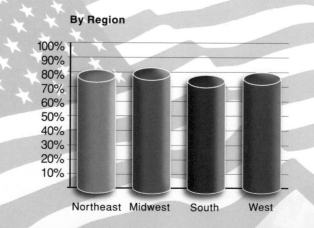

By Region

100%
90%
80%
70%
60%
50%
40%
30%
20%
10%

Northeast   Midwest   South   West

Source: Citizens Flag Alliance, 2005.

A man demonstrates on Capitol Hill to show his support for a constitutional amendment to ban flag burning.

aster or a global conflict. Our history bears that out. The September 11th 2001 attack on America is a prime example of what Americans feel for their flag, and what they know it to be as a symbol of strength, determination and resolve for a free people to remain so.

The Citizens Flag Alliance and The American Legion have done a great deal of polling over the years. The figures are remarkable. Very consistently they have shown that more than three of four Americans want their flag protected. Honestly, I'm surprised the numbers aren't higher. . . .

Some look at the flag and see just a piece of cloth. That perception might be acceptable, but their understanding of the flag's value is lacking. The bits of fabric that make up the flag are only cloth, but when you pull them together in that recognized pattern, something happens. As the flag, it becomes a binding force that holds us together as one people, and those who would desecrate it are out to break that bond. Nothing tears down America more than burning the flag. . . .

Cherishing the Flag

As a nation we are bound together by our shared beliefs. . . . And we are bound by tradition as Americans to pass along to younger generations the importance of upholding those values that are uniquely American. One of the greatest tools for teaching values of respect, commitment, loyalty and patriotism is the Flag of the United States. But how do you explain to a youngster that it's right and customary to respect our flag, but okay to burn it? I have three young children, and I spend time with children all over the country because of my racing activities, and I have no way to explain that to them. . . .

That flag is about values. It's about tradition. It's about America and the men and women who paid an awful price for what we have today.

We honor and cherish members of the Armed Forces and veterans of military service when we honor and protect the flag. Draping the flag over the coffin of a fallen soldier, placing a flag near a grave, or hanging a flag on your house on Memorial Day are all ways we honor and express our appreciation for those who have fought and died defending America. When our laws sanction the physical desecration of the flag the honor is diminished and the recognition is dulled. . . .

The American people deserve the backing of [the Senate] in their desire to protect the flag, and a constitutional amendment [banning flag desecration] to return that right to the people is the only way.

EVALUATING THE AUTHOR'S ARGUMENTS:

In this viewpoint, John Andretti uses persuasive language to support his contention that flag desecration should be banned. Give two examples of this type of language. How does it strengthen Andretti's argument?

Flag Desecration Should Not Be Banned

Russ Feingold

"What kind of symbol of freedom and liberty will our flag be if it has to be protected . . . by a constitutional amendment?"

This viewpoint is excerpted from the congressional testimony of Russ Feingold, a U.S. senator from the state of Wisconsin. Feingold asserts that even though flag desecration is offensive to the majority of Americans, it is an important form of free speech and must be allowed. He is opposed to a constitutional amendment prohibiting flag desecration—something that has been unsuccessfully attempted a number of times in U.S. history—and believes that such an amendment would diminish the civil liberties of Americans. In Feingold's opinion, freedom in the United States is strengthened by tolerance of unpopular forms of speech, including flag desecration.

AS YOU READ, CONSIDER THE FOLLOWING QUESTIONS:
1. What principle has made America a beacon of hope and inspiration, as explained by Feingold?
2. In the author's opinion, what is the best way to explain what America is really about?
3. According to Feingold, how did the September 11, 2001, attacks show that a flag protection amendment is unnecessary?

Russ Feingold, testimony before the U.S. Senate Committee on the Judiciary, Washington, DC, March 10, 2004.

This is [a] hearing . . . on a constitutional amendment [to ban flag desecration]. The amendment . . . would for the first time write discrimination into our Constitution. We are discussing an amendment that would, for the first time, amend the Bill of Rights.[1] Make no mistake, we are talking here today about amending the Constitution of the United States to permit the government to criminalize conduct that, however misguided, is clearly expressive, and is often undertaken as a form of political protest. Adopting this amendment would be a grave mistake.

Not a single Senator who opposes the proposed constitutional amendment, as I do, supports burning or otherwise showing disrespect to the flag. Not a single one. None of us think it's "OK" to burn the flag. None of us view the flag as "just a piece of cloth." On those rare occasions when some malcontent defiles or burns our flag, I join everyone on this dais, and in this room, and in this country, who condemns that action.

FAST FACT

In 1984 at the Republican National Convention in Texas, Gregory Johnson burned a U.S. flag to protest various policies of the Reagan administration. The U.S. Supreme Court subsequently decided that flag burning was protected by the First Amendment as freedom of expression.

The Importance of the Right to Free Expression

At the same time, whatever the political cost, I will defend the right of Americans to express their views about their government, however hateful or spiteful or disrespectful, without fear of their government putting them in jail for those views. America is not a nation of symbols, it is a nation of principles. And the most important principle of all, the principle that has made this country the beacon of hope and inspiration for oppressed peoples throughout the world, is the right of free expression. This amendment, well-intentioned as it may be, threatens that right, and I must oppose it.

I respectfully disagree with the supporters of the amendment about the effect that this issue has on our children. We can send no better,

---

1. As of this writing, an amendment to ban flag desecration had not been passed by Congress.

**DATORY
TRIOTISM
O WAY!**

VIETNAM VETS AGAINST THE WAR
ANTI - IMPERIALIST

A group of protesters in New York stands over a flag burning on the ground.

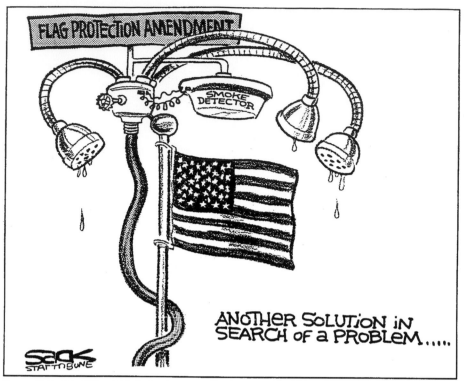

FLAG PROTECTION AMENDMENT

SMOKE DETECTOR

ANOTHER SOLUTION IN SEARCH OF A PROBLEM.....

Sack
STAR TRIBUNE

Source: Sack. © by Tribune Media Services, Inc. All rights reserved. Reproduced by permission.

no stronger, no more meaningful message to our children about the principles and the values of this country than if we explain to them that the beauty and the strength of this country is in its freedoms, not in its symbols. When we uphold First Amendment freedoms despite the efforts of misguided and despicable people who want to provoke our wrath, we explain what America is really about. Our country and our people are far too strong to be threatened by those who burn the flag. That is a lesson worth teaching our children.

An Amendment Is Unnecessary

Amending the First Amendment so we can bring the full wrath of the criminal law and the power of the state down on political dissenters will only encourage more people who want to grandstand their dissent and imagine themselves "martyrs for the cause." We all know what will happen the minute this amendment goes into force—more flag burnings and other despicable acts of disrespect to the flag, not fewer. Will the new law deter these acts? Of course not. Will the amendment make these acts any more despicable than they are today? Certainly not. Will it make us love the flag any more than we do today? Absolutely not.

It was just under four years ago, in 2000, another Presidential election year, that the Senate rejected this constitutional amendment. I would like to hear from our witnesses what has changed in the last four years. Have we seen an alarming increase in incidents of flag burning? Has there been a marked decrease in patriotism or the proud display of the flag on national holidays? Have the armed forces seen a huge drop in enlistment or have soldiers faced disrespectful protests of the sacrifices they and their families make? Of course not.

I venture to say, Mr. President, that outward displays of patriotism are on the rise since we last considered this amendment. We all know why that is. Our country was attacked on September 11th [2001]. And America responded. We didn't need a constitutional amendment

Demonstrators burn a flag in Washington, D.C., during the inauguration of President George W. Bush in 2001.

to teach our citizens how to love their country. They showed us how to do it by hurling themselves into burning buildings to save their fellow citizens who were in danger, by standing in line for hours to give blood, by driving hundreds of miles to search through the rubble for survivors and help in cleanup efforts, by praying in their houses of worship for the victims of the attacks and their families. September 11th inspired our citizens to perform some of the most selfless acts of bravery and patriotism we have seen in our entire history. No constitutional amendment could ever match those acts as a demonstration of patriotism, or create them in the future.

A Symbol of Liberty

In 1999, the late Senator John Chafee, one of this country's greatest war heroes at Gaudalcanal and in the Korean War, testified against this amendment. He said: "We cannot mandate respect and pride in the flag. In fact, . . . taking steps to require citizens to respect the flag, sullies its significance and symbolism." Senator Chafee's words still bring to us a brisk, cool wind of caution. What kind of symbol of freedom and liberty will our flag be if it has to be protected from protesters by a constitutional amendment? I will proudly defend our Constitution against this ill-advised effort to amend it.

EVALUATING THE AUTHORS' ARGUMENTS:

Russ Feingold and John Andretti both believe that the American flag symbolizes freedom, but they disagree on whether flag desecration is a threat to that freedom. If you were to write an essay about flag desecration, what would be your opinion? List three main points you would make to support your point of view.

Media Content Should Be Restricted to Protect Children

Jonathan S. Adelstein

"There is nearly universal concern about the state of our public airwaves."

Jonathan S. Adelstein is a commissioner for the Federal Communications Commission (FCC), the federal agency responsible for regulating broadcast media. In 2004 the FCC began to more strictly regulate broadcast indecency. The following viewpoint is excerpted from Adelstein's congressional testimony in which he defends the FCC's actions. Indecent material has proliferated in broadcast media, says Adelstein. In his opinion this material, which includes violence and sexual content, is inappropriate for children and should be restricted for their protection.

AS YOU READ, CONSIDER THE FOLLOWING QUESTIONS:

1. How many American children were watching the 2004 Super Bowl, according to Adelstein?
2. In the author's opinion, how does the public feel about sex, violence, and profanity in the media?
3. What has no place in broadcasting, according to Adelstein?

Jonathan S. Adelstein, testimony before the U.S. Senate Committee on Commerce, Science, and Transportation, and U.S. House Subcommittee on Telecommunications and the Internet, Washington, DC, February 11, 2004.

L ike many of you, I sat down with my wife and children to watch the Super Bowl [in 2004]. I was expecting a showcase of America's best talent, both on and off the field, and the apotheosis of our cultural creativity during the entertainment and advertising portions. Instead, like millions of others, I was appalled by the halftime show—not just for the shock-value stunt at the end [when singer Janet Jackson's bare breast was revealed] but for the overall raunchy performance displayed in front of so many children—one in five American children were watching, according to reports. And the advertising set a new low for what should air during family time.

The Super Bowl is a rare occasion for families to get together to enjoy a national pastime everyone should be able to appreciate. Instead, a special family occasion was truly disrespected.

Many people were shocked by an incident televised during the 2004 Super Bowl in which Janet Jackson's bare breast was exposed during a performance with Justin Timberlake.

Inappropriate for Children

I could highlight any number of tasteless commercials that depicted sexual and bodily functions in a vile manner. Any sense of internal controls appeared out the window, so long as the advertiser paid the multi-million dollar rate.

One commercial that really stung my family, and many other parents with whom I spoke, was a violent trailer for an unrated horror movie. It showed horrible monsters with huge fangs attacking people. I literally jumped out of my chair to get between the TV and my three-year-old. Other parents told me they couldn't reach for the remote control fast enough. I wonder how those who chose to broadcast such violence can sleep at night when they gave so many American children nightmares.

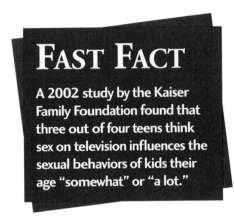

FAST FACT

A 2002 study by the Kaiser Family Foundation found that three out of four teens think sex on television influences the sexual behaviors of kids their age "somewhat" or "a lot."

No parent should have to jump in front of the TV to block their children from such images, whether during a commercial or a halftime show. No parent should feel guilty for not being with their child every single moment in case they need to block the TV during what most would consider to be a family viewing event. . . .

Widespread Concern

This latest incident is only the tip of the iceberg. There is nearly universal concern about the state of our public airwaves. I personally received more than 10,000 emails and the FCC [Federal Communications Commission] received more than 200,000. But that pales in comparison to the number of people who over the past year expressed their outrage to me about the homogenization and crassness of the media. The public is outraged by the increasingly crude content they see and hear in their media today. They are fed up with the sex, violence, and profanity flooding into our homes. . . .

Complaints are exploding that our airwaves are increasingly dominated by graphic and shocking entertainment. Some observe that broadcasters are only responding to competition from cable programming. Take MTV [Music Television], a cable network known for pushing the envelope. It's owned by Viacom, which also owns CBS [television network that broadcast the Super Bowl]. It's no coincidence that MTV produced the halftime show. But the network thoughtlessly applied the cable programmer's standards during the Super Bowl—the ultimate family event.

Indecent Content Must Be Restricted

As a musician, I recognize that channels like MTV have a place in our society. I also understand and respect that many would prefer that they not intrude into the mainstream of American family life. Parents who purchase cable television have the legal right to block any channel they don't consider appropriate for their children. More parents should be made aware of this right. Free over-the-air broadcasting, however, offers no such alternative to parents. For broadcast material designed for mature audiences, it's a matter of the right time and place.

Enough is enough. As a parent and an FCC Commissioner, I share the public's disgust with increasingly crude radio and television content.

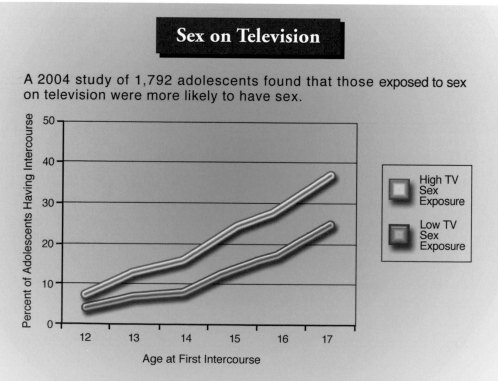

Sex on Television

A 2004 study of 1,792 adolescents found that those exposed to sex on television were more likely to have sex.

Percent of Adolescents Having Intercourse

High TV Sex Exposure

Low TV Sex Exposure

Age at First Intercourse

Source: Rebecca L. Collins et al., *Pediatrics*, September 3, 2004.

The Federal Communications Commission, shown here in session, is charged with regulating the content of the media.

I've only served on the Commission for about a year,[1] but I'm proud that we've stepped up our enforcement in that time. And we need to ramp it up even further. In my view, gratuitous use of swear words or nudity have no place in broadcasting. . . .

Protecting Children

It may very well take more than the FCC to turn this around. We are not the only ones with a public trust to keep the airwaves free from obscene, indecent and profane material. Broadcasters are given exclusive rights to use the public airwaves in the public interest. The broadcasters themselves bear much of the responsibility to keep our airwaves decent. As stewards of the airwaves, broadcasters are in the position to step up and use their public airwaves in a manner that celebrates our country's tremendous cultural heritage. Or they can continue down the path of debasing that heritage. Their choices ultimately will guide our enforcement.

1. Adelstein was appointed to the Commission in 2002, and continues to serve as of this writing.

Serving local communities is the cornerstone of the broadcaster's social compact with the public. When people choose to become licensed broadcasters, they understand that a public service responsibility comes with that privilege. In his famous remarks lamenting the "vast wasteland" of television, [former FCC chairman] Newton Minow rightly observed that, "an investment in broadcasting is buying a share in public responsibility." Every broadcaster should take that to heart. Public responsibility may mean passing up an opportunity to pander to the nation's whims and current ratings trends when it is more important to stand up and meet the needs of the local community. . . .

During the Super Bowl, and on far too many other occasions, people feel assaulted by what is broadcast at them. My job is to protect our families from the broadcast of obscene, indecent or profane material. That also means promoting healthy fare for our children. After all, the airwaves are owned by the American people, and the public is eager to take some control back.

EVALUATING THE AUTHOR'S ARGUMENTS:

Many people argue that parents, not government, should take the role of protecting children from indecent material in the media. In the viewpoint you just read however, Jonathan S. Adelstein argues that government regulation is essential as well. After reading this viewpoint, do you think that parents need government help in monitoring their children's media usage? Explain.

VIEWPOINT 4

Children Do Not Need Media Censorship

Judith Levine

"Evidence of the harm of exposure to sexually explicit images or words in childhood is inconclusive, even nonexistent."

The federal agency responsible for regulating broadcast media is the Federal Communications Commission (FCC). In the following viewpoint Judith Levine maintains that strict FCC regulation of indecency for the protection of children is misguided. There is no evidence that exposure to sexual material harms children, she argues. Instead, the evidence actually reveals that information about sex is beneficial to youth. Levine is the author of *Harmful to Minors: The Perils of Protecting Children from Sex*, which won the 2002 Los Angeles Times Book Prize.

AS YOU READ, CONSIDER THE FOLLOWING QUESTIONS:

1. What did the Lockhart Commission conclude about children and erotica, as cited by the author?
2. According to Levine, what did interviews of sex criminals reveal about children and pornography?
3. In the author's opinion, what is the only thing that can challenge bad speech?

Judith Levine, "Is 'Indecency' Harmful to Minors?" *Extra!* September/October 2004, pp. 27–29. Copyright © 2004 by Judith Levine. Reproduced by permission.

"For more than 75 years . . . Congress has entrusted the FCC with protecting children from broadcast indecency," the Federal Communications Commission's chief enforcer David H. Solomon declared in April 2004. "There's no question that the FCC is taking indecency enforcement very seriously these days."

No question indeed. Solomon was referring to the commission's new regulatory enthusiasm—some would call it a crusade—spearheaded by Chair Michael Powell and seconded by Commissioner Michael J. Copps. . . . In a *USA Today* op-ed (2/4/04), Copps issued a clear warning: "I hear daily from Americans fed up with the patently offensive programming invading their homes," he wrote. "The industry can fix the problem voluntarily. If it won't, government may have to halt the race to the bottom."

In his April speech, Solomon crowed about what the government was already doing to protect children. The FCC was enlivening its definition of indecency—"language or material that, in context, depicts or describes, in terms patently offensive as measured by contemporary community standards for the broadcast medium, sexual or excretory organs or activities"—with a broader category of "profanity." In addition to blasphemy (an already questionable concept in a secular nation), the commission would prohibit any "personally reviling epithets naturally tending to provoke violent resentment" or language "so grossly offensive . . . as to amount to a nuisance." The "F-word" would hereafter be considered such a violently resentment-provoking nuisance. . . .

The FCC's new vigor was more than rhetorical. Behind it, both houses of the Republican Congress had rammed through bills to raise fines for indecency from the current maximum of $27,500 to as high as a half-million dollars; the laws would also revoke broadcast licenses after "three strikes." George W. Bush gave the proposals two thumbs up.

And, oh yes, stressed Solomon, the FCC "remains strongly committed" to the First Amendment. . . .

"Traps for the Young"

The concept of indecency is inextricably linked to protecting children, which is why most sexual speech is prohibited on radio and commercial television between 6 A.M. and 10 P.M., when minors are more likely to be in the audience. According to veteran civil liberties

As the former head of the Federal Communications Commission, Michael Powell worked to protect children from indecent broadcasting.

attorney Marjorie Heins, laws are routinely passed and upheld in court based on the notion that witnessing sexual words and images is harmful to minors. Even among those who challenge the laws' free-speech infringements, few question this truism.

The idea that young (or female or feeble) minds are vulnerable to media-induced bad thoughts, which might lead to bad acts, may be the founding principle of obscenity law. In 1868, an English anti-clerical pamphlet entitled "The Confessional Unmasked" was deemed punishably obscene because its text might "suggest to the minds of the young of either sex, and even to persons of more advanced years, thoughts of a most impure and libidinous character."

In the late 19th Century, while [censorship advocate] Anthony Comstock scoured daily newspapers for censorable "traps for the young," the New York Society for the Prevention of Cruelty to Children "kept a watchful eye upon the so-called Museums of the City," whose advertisements were "like magnets to curious children.". . .

And in 1934, Dr. Ira S. Wile indicted "lurid movies, automobiles, speed, jazz [and] literature tinged with pornography" among the causes of "The Sexual Problems of Adolescence."

After jazz came comic books, then rock 'n' roll, hip-hop, video games, Internet porn—it's a miracle anyone has survived childhood with sufficient morality to protect the next generation from corruption.

The Fantasy of Innocence

In spite of all this hand-wringing, evidence of the harm of exposure to sexually explicit images or words in childhood is inconclusive, even nonexistent. The 1970 U.S. Commission on Obscenity and Pornography, the "Lockhart Commission," failed to find harm to children in view-

Protesters in Washington, D.C., demand more stringent government regulation of online content to restrict the accessibility of pornography to children.

ing erotica, and even suggested such exposure could "facilitate much needed communication between parent and child over sexual matters."

In a survey of 3,200 elementary school kids in the 1970s (before MTV [Music Television]!), "the most productive responses were elicited with the instructions, 'Why children shouldn't be allowed to see R- and X-rated movies'; or 'What is in R- and X-rated movies that children are too young to know about?'" wrote the psychologists who conducted the study. "Here, the children proceeded with aplomb to tell all that they knew but were not supposed to know." The authors' conclusion: Children are sexual, they know about sex and this does not harm them. Their "innocence" is an adult fantasy.

FAST FACT

According to a 2002 report by the Kaiser Family Foundation, even when Internet filters were set on the least restrictive setting, around 9 percent of Web sites that came up when searching for "safe sex" or "condom" were erroneously overblocked. This percent increased to over 50 percent on the most restrictive setting.

Assembled to overturn the 1970 findings, the Reagan Administration's 1985 Commission on Pornography (the "Meese Commission") could not establish factual links between sexually explicit materials and antisocial behavior either. The lion's share of the testimony it heard concerned adult consumers, yet the commission pitched its pro-restriction recommendations to popular fears about children: "For children to be taught by these materials that sex is public, that sex is commercial, and that sex can be divorced from any degree of affection, love, commitment or marriage," the report read, "is for us the wrong message at the wrong time."

Indeed, some research suggests that less exposure to sexual materials may be worse for children than more. Interviews of sex criminals including child molesters reveal that the children who eventually became rapists were usually less exposed to pornography than other kids. In general, according to Johns Hopkins University sexologist John Money, "the majority of patients with paraphilias"—deviant sexual fantasies and behaviors—"described a strict anti-sexual upbringing in which sex was either never mentioned or was actively repressed or defiled."

In the 1980s Edwin Meese headed a commission to identify links between pornography and antisocial behavior. The commission's findings were inconclusive.

On a less criminal note, students who attend sex-ed classes where a wide range of sexual topics are discussed do far better than those in abstinence-only classes when it comes to protecting themselves against pregnancy and disease and negotiating sexual relationships. . . .

The Benefits of Information

It is unlikely the air will get less dense with information, or with sex. No law, no Internet filter or vigilant parent can keep tabs on every pixel that passes before a child's eyes. All adults can do is help kids understand and negotiate the sexual world.

But the campaign against indecency is bigger than children. Parents Television Council and their allies in and outside government would like to bowdlerize the public sphere entirely. So far, the courts have limited attempts, such as numerous online decency statutes, that would reduce all communications to a level appropriate to the Teletubbies [television show].

Still, it is wrong to see censorship as bad for adults and good for children. Everyone can benefit from abundant accurate, realistic sexual information and diverse narratives and images of bodies and sex. In sex as in politics, only more speech can challenge bad speech. We won't all agree on what is bad, but it is time to wrest those definitions from the hands of radical moralists.

EVALUATING THE AUTHORS' ARGUMENTS:

Judith Levine and Jonathan S. Adelstein make opposing arguments about whether media should be censored for children. For each author, list the three most persuasive pieces of support given. Based on their support, which author makes the most persuasive case about media censorship? Why?

VIEWPOINT
5

Internet Filters Should Be Used in Libraries

Supreme Court of the United States

"The interest in protecting young library users from material inappropriate for minors is . . . compelling."

The Children's Internet Protection Act (CIPA), passed in 2000, requires libraries that receive federal funding to install Internet filters on their computers to protect children from indecent material. The following viewpoint is excerpted from a 2003 decision of the U.S. Supreme Court, reaffirming the constitutionality of CIPA. The Court explains that filters are the best way for libraries to ensure that children can access educational material on the Internet, but also be protected from harmful material such as pornography. It explains that this does not unfairly compromise the free speech rights of adults because they can request that librarians disable these filters. The Supreme Court is the highest court in the United States.

AS YOU READ, CONSIDER THE FOLLOWING QUESTIONS:
1. What is the traditional mission of libraries, according to the author?
2. As explained by the Court, why do libraries provide Internet access?
3. What type of material have libraries traditionally excluded from their collections?

U.S. Supreme Court, *United States et al. v. American Library Association, Inc. et al.,* Washington, DC, June 23, 2003.

Two forms of federal assistance help public libraries provide patrons with Internet access: discounted rates under the E-rate program and grants under the Library Services and Technology Act (LSTA). Upon discovering that library patrons, including minors, regularly search the Internet for pornography and expose others to pornographic images by leaving them displayed on Internet terminals or printed at library printers, Congress enacted the Children's Internet Protection Act (CIPA), which forbids public libraries to receive federal assistance for Internet access unless they install software to block obscene or pornographic images and to prevent minors from accessing material harmful to them. . . .

Consistent with Library Goals

To fulfill their traditional missions of facilitating learning and cultural enrichment, public libraries must have broad discretion to decide what material to provide to their patrons. . . . Internet terminals are not acquired by a library in order to create a public forum for Web publishers to express themselves. Rather, a library provides such access for the same reasons it offers other library resources: to facilitate research,

Source: Asay. © by Creators Syndicate, Inc. Reproduced by permission.

learning, and recreational pursuits by furnishing materials of requisite and appropriate quality. The fact that a library reviews and affirmatively chooses to acquire every book in its collection, but does not review every Web site that it makes available, is not a constitutionally relevant distinction. The decisions by most libraries to exclude pornography from their print collections are not subjected to heightened scrutiny; it would make little sense to treat libraries' judgments to block online pornography any differently. Moreover, because of the vast quantity of material on the Internet and the rapid pace at which it changes, libraries cannot possibly segregate, item by item, all the Internet material that is appropriate for inclusion from all that is not. While a library could limit its Internet collection to just those sites it found worthwhile, it could do so only at the cost of excluding an enormous amount of valuable information that it lacks the capacity to review. Given that tradeoff, it is entirely reasonable for public libraries to reject that approach and instead exclude certain categories of content, without making individualized judgments that everything made available has requisite and appropriate quality. Concerns over filtering software's tendency to erroneously "overblock" access to constitutionally protected speech that falls outside the categories software users intend to block are dispelled by the ease with which patrons may have the filtering software disabled.

FAST FACT

According to a 2002 survey by the London School of Economics, nine out of ten children aged between eight and sixteen have viewed pornography on the Internet. In most cases, the sex sites were accessed unintentionally, often in the process of doing homework.

Not a Violation of Free Speech

CIPA does not impose an unconstitutional condition on libraries that receive E-rate and LSTA subsidies by requiring them, as a condition on that receipt, to surrender their First Amendment right to provide the public with access to constitutionally protected speech. . . . The Government here is not denying a benefit to anyone, but is instead simply insisting that public funds be spent for the purpose for which they

Library patrons access the Internet. In 2003 the Supreme Court upheld CIPA, an act that requires federally funded libraries to install Internet filters.

Librarians can instruct their adult patrons on how to override Internet filtering software.

are authorized: helping public libraries fulfill their traditional role of obtaining material of requisite and appropriate quality for educational and informational purposes. Especially because public libraries have traditionally excluded pornographic material from their other collections, Congress could reasonably impose a parallel limitation on its Internet assistance programs. As the use of filtering software helps to carry out these programs, it is a permissible condition. . . .

The interest in protecting young library users from material inappropriate for minors is legitimate, and even compelling. . . .

The Best Solution

No clearly superior or better fitting alternative to Internet software filters has been presented. Moreover, the statute contains an important exception that limits the speech-related harm: It allows libraries to permit any adult patron access to an "overblocked" Web site or to disable the software filter entirely upon request. Given the comparatively small burden imposed upon library patrons seeking legitimate Internet materials, it cannot be said that any speech-related harm that the statute may cause is disproportionate when considered in relation to the statute's legitimate objectives.

EVALUATING THE AUTHOR'S ARGUMENTS:

While the First Amendment to the U.S. Constitution protects freedom of speech, many people, such as the author of this viewpoint, argue that some censorship of speech is necessary for the protection of children. After reading the viewpoints in this chapter, do you believe that the First Amendment should apply differently to children than adults? Why or why not?

VIEWPOINT

6

Internet Filters Should Not Be Used in Libraries

J.J. Hysell

"Filters can keep vital information under wraps."

In 2000 the Child's Internet Protection Act was passed, requiring libraries that receive federal funding to install Internet filters on their computers. In a 2003 decision, the U.S. Supreme Court upheld the constitutionality of the act. Many people, however, continue to argue that library filters are a threat to free speech. In the following newspaper editorial, J.J. Hysell makes this argument, asserting that filters are not the best way to protect children from obscene material and that they also block important nonpornographic material. In addition, argues Hysell, while it is theoretically easy for adults to request that filters be unblocked, it is often embarrassing for them to do so.

AS YOU READ, CONSIDER THE FOLLOWING QUESTIONS:
1. As explained by the author, what type of educational sites might filters block?
2. In Hysell's opinion, how do communities benefit from library computers?
3. Why are violations of the use of library computers rare, according to the author?

J.J. Hysell, "To Filter or Not to Filter?" *Solares Hill,* vol. 26, June 27, 2003, p. 4. Copyright © 2005 by ProQuest Information and Learning Company. All rights reserved. Reproduced by permission.

The Supreme Court ruled that it has lost all faith in one of the last remaining forms of the honor system. Well, that's not exactly how it explained a recent ruling but it might as well have hung a sign on every library door saying, "Quiet! Censorship spoken here." With its recent decision, the court tightened the belt on First Amendment rights when it ordered libraries to install pornography filters on public-use computers—or face the loss of federal funding.

The Reality of Internet Filters

The court ruled that the Children's Internet Protection Act (CIPA) is constitutional, which means libraries are now faced with the job—and financial burden—of equipping their systems with site-blocking software. The idea is a noble one, based on the concept of protecting minors from viewing what they don't need to see, but the reality is not so morally quaint.

In 2003 the U.S. Supreme Court ruled that federally funded public libraries must install software to filter pornography in order to prevent minors from accessing indecent material.

What a perfect way to endanger the declining quality of public libraries. Although it certainly is the answer to keeping youths from viewing smut on the internet, why is it suddenly the responsibility of the libraries and not parents and educators?

While some filters can be useful in a home atmosphere, they are not a quickly-applicable band-aid made to cover what society deems as its wounds. Most filters block access to pornographic sites, but some

Many librarians believe that Internet filters give a false sense of security and may actually prevent users from accessing legitimate information.

also tend to block important sites that may be helpful to research or education. For instance, many filters are all-encompassing—reliable sites about breast cancer, AIDS, human rights and sex education are often disabled and therefore inaccessible. Many of the reasons Americans lauded the internet at its inception, citing its freedom from judgment and its versatility, are now jeopardized in the public sphere.

The 6-3 ruling was supposedly smoothed by two justices who said the law would only work if librarians could disable the filters when so requested by adults. That puts the library patron in an even more compromising position. Not only is the information he or she is seeking now deemed "taboo," but a request must be made of a complete stranger to assist in locating facts that, if contained in a book, could be found without the same embarrassment. And there is a permanent record of the request. Grab your scarlet letter at the door.

Filters Block Vital Information

According to Norma Kula, Director of Libraries for Monroe County [Florida], our local library is currently [in 2003] shopping for the best filter; it's been a difficult task.

"We've looked at several and have been dissatisfied with what we've seen so far," Kula said. "Some are difficult to use and are unsatisfactory in what they do."

Kula echoed the concern about how filters can keep vital information under wraps. She gave examples of how "keyword filtering" can overpower a computer. For instance, if the word "breast" is excluded, medical research information could be hidden. If the word "sex" is blocked, geographical information that includes Middlesex County won't be found. Even sports fans looking for statistics from Super Bowl XXX could find themselves in a bind, because the triple X could signal a block.

"The filters give a false sense of security," Kula said.

Kula added that children's computers are separate from the main computers and are supervised at all times. Children cannot access the internet without parental permission and a library staff member present. It is certainly appropriate to block sites when dealing with computer access for young people, and the goal is to educate both the parent and the child together on using the internet in a positive way.

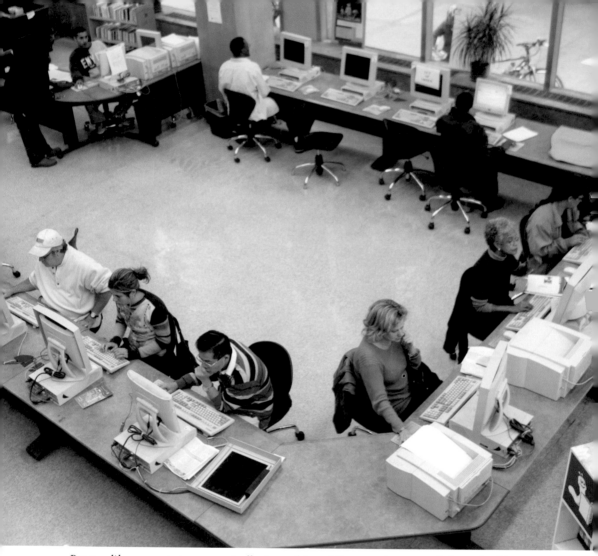

Because library computers are typically situated in public spaces, instances of abuse of public Internet access are rare.

A Threat to Free Speech

The crux of the debate about filters centers on how adults should be able to make their own decisions concerning free speech.

Many librarians across the country are seething. But where does that leave the public? According to Associated Press figures, libraries have received nearly $1 billion in technology subsidies since 1999. The boost to communities provided by public access to a wealth of timely, valuable information has been substantial. Those who can't afford computers or who need help to use them have found a haven at the library.

Violations of the use of library computers are rare because of the honor system that has defined public libraries since day one. Most libraries require patrons to sign a document assuring they won't use the computer to access suggestive or offensive sites. In addition, most computers are located in plain view of the librarians, who monitor their use. If someone chooses to breach the code of ethics, they will face the wrath of the library staff, as well as fellow patrons and possibly the authorities.

Maybe the justices of the Supreme Court should take a trip to their local library and read up on the First Amendment. They may not find much if they use the internet.

EVALUATING THE AUTHORS' ARGUMENTS:

The right to free speech in the United States is protected by the First Amendment to the Constitution which states that, "Congress shall make no law . . . abridging the freedom of speech." In reality however, certain forms of speech, such as pornography, are often restricted. In your opinion, should limits be placed on freedom of expression? Cite from the viewpoints in this chapter to support your answer.

CHAPTER 2

Does Terrorism Justify Curtailing Civil Liberties?

An armed police officer stands guard in Manhattan on the second anniversary of the September 11, 2001, terrorist attacks.

VIEWPOINT 1

Some Civil Liberties Must Be Sacrificed to Fight Terrorism

Richard A. Posner

"*[Civil liberties] should be curtailed, to the extent that the benefits in greater security outweigh the costs in reduced liberty.*"

Richard A. Posner is a judge for the United States Court of Appeals for the Seventh Circuit and a senior lecturer at the University of Chicago Law School. In the following viewpoint he argues that civil liberties are not an absolute, unchanging right and they must be balanced with national security. Throughout U.S. history, civil liberties have necessarily been reduced in times of crisis, says Posner, because the benefits of greater security outweighed the costs in reduced liberty. In his opinion, in order to effectively protect the United States from terrorism, civil liberties must be reduced.

AS YOU READ, CONSIDER THE FOLLOWING QUESTIONS:

1. As argued by Posner, why did the framers of the Constitution leave most of its provisions on rights pretty vague?
2. How does the author reply to the argument that dangers to national security have historically been exaggerated?
3. How can the United States minimize the net decreases in civil liberties, according to Posner?

Richard A. Posner, "The Truth About Our Liberties," *Responsive Community*, vol. 12, Summer 2002, pp. 4–7.
Copyright © 2002 by Richard A. Posner. Reproduced by permission.

In the wake of the September 11 [2001] terrorist attacks have come many proposals for tightening security; some measures to that end have already been taken. Civil libertarians are troubled. They fear that concerns about national security will lead to an erosion of civil liberties. They offer historical examples of supposed overreactions to threats to national security. They treat our existing civil liberties—freedom of the press, protections of privacy and of the rights of criminal suspects, and the rest—as sacrosanct, insisting that the battle against international terrorism accommodate itself to them.

A Fluid Approach to Civil Liberties

I consider this a profoundly mistaken approach to the question of balancing liberty and security. The basic mistake is the prioritizing of liberty. It is a mistake about law and a mistake about history. Let me begin with law. What we take to be our civil liberties—for example, immunity from arrest except upon probable cause to believe we've committed a crime, and from prosecution for violating a criminal statute enacted after we committed the act that violates it—were made legal rights by the Constitution and other enactments. The other enactments can be changed relatively easily, by amendatory legislation. Amending the Constitution is much more difficult. In recognition of this the Framers left most of the constitutional provisions that confer rights pretty vague. The courts have made them definite.

Concretely, the scope of these rights has been determined, through an interaction of constitutional text and subsequent judicial interpretation, by a weighing of competing interests. I'll call them the public-safety interest and the liberty interest. Neither, in my view, has priority. They are both important, and their relative importance changes from time to time and from situation to situation. The safer

FAST FACT

In 2004 Attorney General John Ashcroft stated that the Patriot Act had helped convict 195 individuals of terrorism-related actions.

Judge Richard A. Posner believes that civil liberties must be curtailed in times of crisis.

the nation feels, the more weight judges will be willing to give to the liberty interest. The greater the threat that an activity poses to the nation's safety, the stronger will the grounds seem for seeking to repress that activity even at some cost to liberty. This fluid approach is only common sense.

Protesters in New York denounce Attorney General John Ashcroft and the Patriot Act.

Security Outweighs Liberty

If it is true, therefore, as it appears to be at this writing, that the events of September 11 have revealed the United States to be in much greater jeopardy from international terrorism than had previously been believed—have revealed it to be threatened by a diffuse, shadowy enemy that must be fought with police measures as well as military force—it stands to reason that our civil liberties will be curtailed. They should be curtailed, to the extent that the benefits in greater security outweigh the costs in reduced liberty. All that can reasonably be asked of the responsible legislative and judicial officials is that they weigh the costs as carefully as the benefits.

It will be argued that the lesson of history is that officials habitually exaggerate dangers to the nation's security. But the lesson of history is the opposite. It is because officials have repeatedly and disastrously underestimated these dangers that our history is as violent as it is. Consider such underestimated dangers as that of secession, which led to the Civil War;

of a Japanese attack on the United States, which led to the disaster at Pearl Harbor; of Soviet espionage in the 1940s, which accelerated the Soviet Union's acquisition of nuclear weapons and emboldened [former Soviet Union leader Joseph] Stalin to encourage North Korea's invasion of South Korea; of the installation of Soviet missiles in Cuba, which precipitated the Cuban missile crisis; of political assassinations and outbreaks of urban violence in the 1960s; of the Tet Offensive of 1968; of the Iranian revolution of 1979 and the subsequent taking of American diplomats as hostages; and, for that matter, of the events of September 11.

Sacrificing Legality for Security

It is true that when we are surprised and hurt, we tend to overreact—but only with the benefit of hindsight can a reaction be separated into its proper and excess layers. In hindsight we know that interning Japanese Americans did not shorten World War II. But was this known at the time? If not, shouldn't the Army have erred on the side of caution, as it did? Even today we cannot say with any assurance that Abraham Lincoln was wrong to suspend habeas corpus during the Civil War, as he did on several occasions, even though the Constitution is clear that only Congress can suspend this right. (Another of Lincoln's wartime measures, the Emancipation Proclamation, may also have been unconstitutional.) But Lincoln would have been wrong to cancel the 1864 presidential election, as some urged: by November of 1864 the North was close to victory, and canceling the election would have created a more dangerous precedent than the wartime suspension of habeas corpus.[1] This last example shows that civil liberties remain part of the balance even in the most dangerous of times, and even though their relative weight must then be less.

Lincoln's unconstitutional acts during the Civil War show that even legality must sometimes be sacrificed for other values. We are a nation under law, but first we are a nation. I want to emphasize something else, however: the malleability of law, its pragmatic rather than dogmatic character. The law is not absolute, and the slogan "*Fiat iustitia rat caelum*" ("Let justice be done though the heavens fall") is dangerous nonsense. The law is a human creation rather than a divine gift, a tool of government rather

---

1. The 1864 election was conducted in the middle of the Civil War. By suspending habeas corpus prior to the election, Lincoln was able to arrest many of his opponents and prevent them from voting against him.

In the post-9/11 world, most travelers recognize the need for heightened airport security.

than a mandarin mystery. It is an instrument for promoting social welfare, and as the conditions essential to that welfare change, so must it change.

Minimize the Decrease in Civil Liberties

Civil libertarians today are missing something else—the opportunity to challenge other public-safety concerns that impair civil liberties. I have particularly in mind the war on drugs. The sale of illegal drugs is a "victimless" crime in the special but important sense that it is a consensual activity. Usually there is no complaining witness, so in order to bring the criminals to justice the police have to rely heavily on paid informants (often highly paid and often highly unsavory), undercover agents, wiretaps and other forms of electronic surveillance, elaborate sting operations, the infiltration of suspect organizations, random searches, the monitoring of airports and highways, the "profiling" of likely suspects on the basis of ethnic or racial identity or national origin, compulsory drug tests, and other intrusive methods that put pressure on civil liberties. The war on drugs has been a big flop; moreover, in light of what September 11 has taught us about the gravity of the terrorist threat to the United States, it becomes hard to take entirely seriously the threat to the nation that drug use is said to pose. Perhaps it is time to redirect law-enforcement resources from the investigation and apprehension of drug dealers to the investigation and apprehension of international terrorists. By doing so we may be able to minimize the net decrease in our civil liberties that the events of September 11 have made inevitable.

EVALUATING THE AUTHORS' ARGUMENTS:

The author of this viewpoint argues that civil liberties increase and decrease according to whether the security of the United States is threatened. The author of the next viewpoint contends that decreases in civil liberties are often permanent. What evidence does each author use to support his argument? Which point of view do you find most convincing? Explain.

In 1918 President Woodrow Wilson passed the Sedition Act, which was designed to punish those who openly criticize the government during wartime.

United States, or the military or naval forces of the United States, or the flag of the United States, or the uniform of the Army or Navy of the United Sates into contempt, scorn, contumely, or disrepute." Nor was this all the statute forbade!

When convictions under the Sedition Act were challenged in the courts, the U.S. Supreme Court upheld the statute. To his eternal shame, Justice Oliver Wendell Holmes, Jr., wrote: "When a nation is at war, many things that might be said in time of peace are such a hindrance to its effort that their utterance will not be endured so long as men fight and no Court could regard them as protected by any constitutional right." This decision and others upholding unconstitutional measures undertaken by the Wilson administration might strike the proverbial Man from Mars as odd, because the Constitution itself makes no provision for its own evisceration during wartime or other crisis, yet time and again during national emergencies the justices have allowed the legislative branch and especially the executive branch of government to transcend their constitutionally enumerated powers and to nullify individual rights proclaimed in the Constitution.

The Wilson administration conscripted some 2.8 million men—70 percent of those who served in the army. The Supreme Court could find no constitutional infirmity in that involuntary servitude, and its ruling has been a decisive precedent for judges ever since. The government also intervened massively in economic affairs, setting prices, allocating raw materials, and even going so far as to nationalize the interstate railroad, ocean shipping, and telecommunications industries. Those measures established precedents that would return to haunt subsequent generations and undercut their liberties in later crises—economic depressions as well as wars—each time entering more deeply into the fiber of American life, with malign effects on the traditional American devotion to liberty.

World War II Restrictions

World War II became the occasion for unprecedented repressive actions by the U.S. government. More than 10 million young men—about 63 percent of all those who served in the armed forces during the war—were drafted to fight, and hundreds of thousands of them died or suffered serious wounds. The government imprisoned nearly 6,000 conscientious objectors, most of them Jehovah's Witnesses, who refused to obey the conscription laws. Totally without due process of law, the government confined some 112,000 innocent persons of Japanese ancestry, most of them U.S. citizens, in concentration camps in desolate areas of the west. Perceived enemies of FDR's [former U.S. president Franklin Delano Roosevelt's] administration came under surveillance by the FBI [Federal Bureau of Investigation] whose special-agent ranks mushroomed from 785 to 4,370 during the war.

The government built a massive apparatus of economic controls between 1941 and 1945 and displaced free markets for the duration. No one should pooh-pooh the wartime economic controls because they entailed a sacrifice of "mere" economic liberties, as opposed to "precious" civil liberties. Men were sent to prison for violating price controls, and people were displaced from their homes to make way for military construction projects. Wartime taxation itself was no trivial assault.

To pay for the gargantuan munitions production, the government imposed new taxes and raised the rates of existing taxes to unprecedented heights. Payroll withholding of income taxes was instituted,

World War II draftees take an oath of service in 1943. Draftees who refused to serve were imprisoned.

Source: Rogers. © by *The Pittsburgh Post-Gazette*. Reproduced by permission of United Feature Syndicate, Inc.

as portentous an action as any, because it created a virtually automatic means of snatching people's earnings and thereby greatly facilitated the government's subsequent financing of its ever-growing expenditures. Despite the vastly increased taxation, the government had to borrow most of its wartime revenue, and the national debt swelled by $200 billion (equivalent to roughly ten times that amount in today's dollars), or about fivefold, creating liabilities that would hover over taxpayers ever afterward.

Lasting Effects

World War II gave a tremendous fillip to the federal government's reputation as a "can-do" organization, which helped to sustain various wartime economic controls, most notoriously New York City's never-abandoned rent controls. Moreover, as economist Calvin Hoover observed, the war "conditioned [American businessmen] to accept a degree of governmental intervention and control after the war which they had deeply resented prior to it."

During the prolonged Cold War emergency, an apprehensive nation grew accustomed to extensive domestic surveillance, government infiltration of dissident political groups, and even the murder of persons perceived by the government as threats to "national security." In the light of these and countless other facts, one wonders how Winik managed to conclude that "our democracy can, and has, outlived temporary restrictions and continued to thrive"?

Winik would have us believe that, even if the government should adopt much more repressive measures to fight its declared "war on terrorism"—and indeed it has done so since his article appeared—we shall ultimately get past them, back to our glorious democracy, with the dangers surmounted and our freedoms undiminished. Vice President Dick Cheney, however, sees the matter in a different light. The present war "may never end," Cheney said on October 19 [2001]. "It's a new normalcy."

In the weeks that have passed since the Vice President uttered those ominous words, the government has continued to act in ways that confirm the worst fears of those who cherish a free society. Many of the measures being taken will have little effect on terrorism but much effect on ordinary Americans, and many of those measures will surely persist even when the present crisis has passed.

EVALUATING THE AUTHOR'S ARGUMENTS:

What examples does Robert Higgs use to back up his argument that civil liberties should not be sacrificed in times of crisis? Which example do you find the most convincing? Least convincing?

Racial Profiling Should Be Used to Prevent Terrorism

Herbert London

"There might be times when we violate someone's civil liberties in order to protect the welfare of this Country."

Common sense dictates that some racial profiling must be used in the war on terrorism, states Herbert London in the following viewpoint. He argues that because most of the September 11, 2001, terrorists were from Saudi Arabia and were radical Islamists, it is statistically likely that future terrorists might also share these characteristics. Thus, in his opinion, it makes sense for law enforcement to more closely scrutinize these groups in the effort to prevent terrorism. London believes that while this may represent a violation of civil liberties, it is a sacrifice that must be made in order to protect the welfare of the United States. London is president of the Hudson Institute, a think-tank in Indianapolis, Indiana, and author of *Decade of Denial*.

AS YOU READ, CONSIDER THE FOLLOWING QUESTIONS:

1. As explained by the author, why are statistics frequently used as a basis for decision making?

Herbert London, "Profiling as Needed," *Albany Law Review*, vol. 66, Winter 2002, p. 343. Copyright © 2002 by Albany Law School. Reproduced by permission.

When we talk about eliminating profiling, one must argue that there is profiling that goes on all of the time. All of us are engaged in profiling to one degree or another. For example, [U.S. secretary of transportation] Mr. [Norman] Mineta says that not all Islamic people are terrorists. Indeed, nothing could be more obvious. However, it is also true that people who engage in terror worldwide—whether it is in Bali, at the World Trade Center, or the Pentagon—happen to be radical Islamists. So while we say on the one hand that we are not engaging in profiling—indeed, we do. Common sense would dictate that some form of profiling goes on all of the time in the area of law enforcement even if it is not formal.

Common Sense Profiling

All you have to do is spend a little time at the police department in New York City as I have on numerous occasions. If you are in Washington Heights you know that the cocaine traffic is pretty much controlled by the Dominican population. That is not to suggest that every Dominican is engaged in cocaine trafficking—that is absurd. But it is also very fair to say that cocaine traffic is controlled by Dominicans. On the other hand, the heroin traffic is pretty much controlled by Jamaicans. That is not to argue that every Jamaican is engaged in the heroin traffic. But every cop in Washington Heights would know that if you are going to look for people who are distributing heroin, you are probably better off starting with the Jamaican population.

What does the terrorist attack suggest? Something very similar and equally obvious. Most of the people who engaged in the attack on the United States carried Saudi Arabian passports. Does that mean that everyone in Saudi Arabia is engaged in terrorist acts? Of course not. But it is also true that if you are engaged in law enforcement, one of the first and very obvious things that you would do is look very carefully at someone carrying a Saudi Arabian passport and look who is on an airplane in the United States. . . .

Decisions Based on Statistics

Obviously, statistics are not always reliable. But if you are a law enforcement officer, you prefer not to start an investigation with only randomness—you are trying to find some select group within the population. So, statistics become an empirical basis on which to make decisions.

Let me use New York as an example largely because I reside there. Suppose you are a single female entering the subway at twelve o'clock at night, and the cars are not particularly crowded. One car has [religious

Security personnel monitor people entering the baggage claim area of Dulles Airport. Passengers matching certain profiles are closely observed and often interrogated.

group] Hari Krishna members singing songs, and the other has sixteen-year-olds carrying boom boxes, wearing their baseball caps backwards, and without any laces in their sneakers. Which car do you enter? It is fairly obvious. We engage in some sort of profiling. Is it appropriate? Not always.

If you are a jewelry storeowner, a youngster comes in and rings your bell, and again, he is wearing his baseball cap backwards—you might say "I don't know. He's seventeen years old. Why should I take a chance on a robbery?" If it is an octogenarian female who happens to be white, black, or Chinese, would you open your door? Of course you would. People operate on assumptions all the time. This is merely a matter of common sense.

Security personnel in airports across the United States select passengers at random to undergo a thorough inspection with a metal detector.

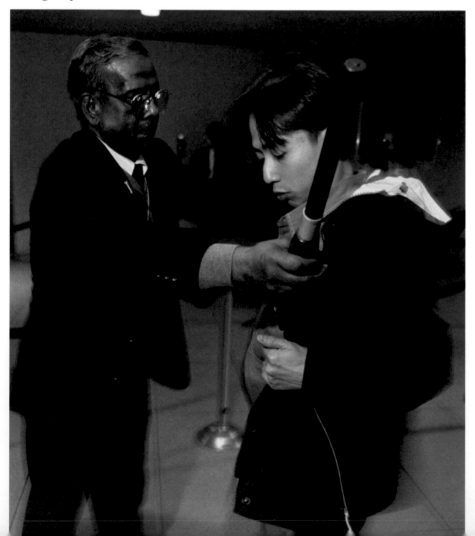

A Necessary Trade-Off

The Japanese relocation camps of World War II were a reprehensible moment in history. . . . However, there was a degree of hysteria in the United States based on the War. After all, Pearl Harbor was seen as a sneak attack on the United States. Moreover, there were also balloons armed with explosives that were sent by Japan to the West Coast of the United States. Here was a situation not entirely different from some of the hysteria that emerged after the attack on the United States on September 11th [2001]. Historical context is critical in evaluating these conditions.

FAST FACT

Immediately following the September 11, 2001, terrorist attacks, a Gallup poll found that 60 percent of Americans wanted Arabs to undergo more intensive screening at airports.

When we are fighting a war, legal positions often change. It is not surprising that [former U.S. president Abraham] Lincoln abandoned habeas corpus during the Civil War. Was it appropriate? Looking back over the course of time one might say that it was not. But obviously we are not living in 1860, 1861 or 1862. We are engaged in a freedom-security equation not unlike the conditions that are faced by people in the past. In the freedom-security equation, we have to ask ourselves, if we interrogate or detain one person inappropriately, but in the process save one million lives, is it worth the trade-off? That is precisely the kind of question that we have to face at the moment.

This is not a war like wars of the past. We are not mobilizing millions of Americans to fight, but there is a clear enemy. The enemy is made up of radical Islamists, who not only detest the United States; they detest our culture, and they detest modernity. They are at war with America. It is important to understand the nature of the enemy. This is not Bonnie and Clyde robbing some banks.[1] These people are intent on destroying a significant segment of American life. Are we willing to engage in racial profiling in order to maintain some sense of order and understanding of the American way of life—even if in the process we violate some civil liberties?

---

1. Bonnie Parker and Clyde Barrow robbed numerous banks, stores, and gas stations in the early 1930s.

In 2002 rapper Jam Master Jay was gunned down in his New York recording studio.

Violating Rights to Save Lives

The problem, as I see it, is that the violation of rights is always visible, but saving lives might not be. How do you make a judgment about what is appropriate? If the government goes too far in violating our understanding of Constitutional provisions, we may say it was an inappropriate act. However, if the government goes too far by our standards, but in the process saves a million lives, is that an appropriate trade-off? I ask the question because I think that it is the question for all Americans to ask at this time even though there is no obvious answer. . . .

Let me give you one other illustration. Rapper Jam Master Jay was recently killed [in 2002]. Jason Mizell was his name at birth. Was his death a function of the national violence that so many members of the press have suggested? Was he killed because he lived in a violent society? Or is it more appropriate to say he was probably killed because of an internal war within the rap world? That is not unusual when you consider what happened to Tupac Shakur[2] and a number of other rap artists. Particularistic violence rather than universal violence may be the issue. Is it a question of simply having violence that is endemic to the American society, or is it a violence within this particular community? If you are engaged in law enforcement do you simply say that everyone is culpable because we live in a violent society, or are you more likely to find the people who are responsible for this act within the rap world?

Again, and I probably should end on this note, if we are thinking about September 11th, September 11th represents a significant departure from anything that we have known in our lifetime. It is even more significant than Pearl Harbor because it occurred on the American mainland. It was an attack on the United States. This is a different period during which we have to employ every means at our disposal to foil the efforts of those who are intent on destroying the United States. That is what we are up against. Do we suspend freedoms in order to take care of ourselves and to defend ourselves? Well, certainly I am not in favor of that. But at the same time, I think that we have to recognize that in the freedom-security exchange, there might be times when we violate someone's civil liberties in order to protect the welfare of this Country.

EVALUATING THE AUTHORS' ARGUMENTS:

List two main points that Herbert London makes to prove his case that racial profiling can help prevent another terrorist attack in the United States. How do you think Amnesty International, the author of the next viewpoint, would respond to these arguments?

2. Shakur was fatally shot in 1996. Many people believe that his death was a result of antagonism between him and other rappers.

VIEWPOINT 4

Racial Profiling Should Not Be Used to Prevent Terrorism

Amnesty International

"Reliance on racial profiling has repeatedly led to national security tragedies."

Founded in London in 1961, Amnesty International is a Nobel Prize–winning activist organization that undertakes research and action focused on preventing and ending human rights abuses. In the following viewpoint the organization cites numerous historical examples to prove that racial profiling is an ineffective strategy for fighting terrorism. Not only does it not work, maintains Amnesty International, but when law enforcement officials focus on a particular race, they are likely to miss suspicious behavior by people who do not belong to that race. The organization argues that the most effective way to prevent terrorism is to focus on the traits and behaviors of an individual, not on their race.

AS YOU READ, CONSIDER THE FOLLOWING QUESTIONS:
1. Of the thousands of Japanese Americans detained during World War II, how many were convicted of spying for Japan, according to Amnesty International?

Amnesty International, "Threat and Humiliation: Racial Profiling, Domestic Security, and Human Rights in the United States," www.amnestyusa.org, October 2004. Copyright © 2004 by Amnesty International, USA. Reproduced by permission.

2. Why was Oklahoma City bomber Timothy McVeigh able to flee law enforcement officers repeatedly in 1995, in the author's opinion?
3. According to Amnesty International, what was the result when the U.S. Customs Service eliminated the use of racial profiling techniques in the 1990s?

Racial profiling is a liability in the effort to make our nation safer. Race-based policing practices have frequently distracted law enforcement officials and made them blind to dangerous behaviors and real threats. Moreover, this is a lesson that law enforcement should have internalized a long time ago. To help illustrate the grave cost of racial profiling as an intended guard against acts of international and domestic terror, we offer two historical examples. The first is from the opening of the twentieth century; the second is from the opening of the twenty-first:

President McKinley's Assassination

In September 1901, President [William] McKinley was murdered by Leon Czolgosz, an American-born native of Michigan, who concealed a pistol in a bandage that was wrapped around his arm and hand so it looked like it covered a wound or broken bone. Secret Service agent George Foster was assigned to search individuals coming to the area where President McKinley would be greeting members of the public. He later admitted to having chosen not to search Czolgosz because he was focused on a "dark complexioned man with a black moustache" who was behind Czolgosz in the line of people coming through Foster's checkpoint. Agent Foster tried to explain his actions by telling investigators that the "colored man" made him feel suspicious. When asked "Why?" he replied, "I didn't like his general appearance." Ironically, it was later revealed that the man whose complexion had so captivated the agent's attention was the same person who saved President McKinley from a third bullet and apprehended the assassin— Jim Parker, an African-American former constable who attended the event as a spectator. Mr. Parker's act of heroism was widely credited with extending the President's life for several days. As a result of reliance

Police initially overlooked John Muhammad as a suspect in the 2002 D.C.-area sniper case because he did not conform to their profile of the shooter.

on racial stereotypes, the agent on duty overlooked Czolgosz, who despite his foreign-sounding last name—not to mention his avowed allegiance to the anarchist cause—looked like "a mechanic out for the day to the Exposition."

Washington, DC–Area Sniper Attacks

During the 2002 sniper attacks in the DC area, police officers were looking for a disaffected white man acting alone or with a single accomplice (the standard profile of a serial killer). After several subsequent reports, they focused their search on white males driving white vans. Police officers conducting surveillance and searches throughout the metropolitan area—including those at each of the multiple roadblocks that were quickly put up after most of the shootings—used this general description of the suspect and the suspect's vehicle. At one point, due to mistaken leads about Middle-Eastern terrorists, the FBI began planning to question [terrorist group] Al-Qaeda prisoners held at Guantánamo Bay, Cuba for possible information on the snipers. Meanwhile, police came in contact with the African-American man and boy—who were ultimately accused, tried, and convicted for the crimes—at least ten times and did not apprehend them because, according to DC homicide detective Tony Patterson, "everybody just got tunnel vision." The suspects' blue Chevrolet Caprice was spotted near one of the shooting scenes, and was stopped several times by police, yet the snipers were able to escape every time with the alleged murder weapons in their possession. Officials were so focused on race that they failed to notice that one of the snipers, John Allen Muhammad, possessed many of the other characteristics often associated with serial killers (i.e., military background, angry, divorced, lost custody of children, etc.). As former FBI Agent Candace DeLong put it, "A black sniper? That was the last thing I was thinking."

In each case, the United States paid a clear price for law enforcement officers thinking that they knew what an otherwise unidentified threat looked like. In the first instance, the U.S. president was assassinated, in part, because his Secret Service agents were apparently relying on stereotypes of what an "international anarchist" looked like. In the second, millions of residents of the Washington, DC metropolitan area were terrorized for several days as the serial killers repeatedly evaded police, in part because officers were relying upon scientifically-supported profiles that speculated the assailants were white. As DC Police Chief Charles Ramsey pointed out, "We were looking for a white van with white people, and we ended up with a blue car with black people." In each instance, officers' ability to focus on and detect dangerous behaviors (a pistol in the bandaged hand of a white male passing through a Secret Service checkpoint; a rifle in the

> ## FAST FACT
>
> In an October 2001 Zogby International poll of Arab Americans, 20 percent said they personally had experienced racial discrimination since the September 11 attacks, and 45 percent said they knew someone else who had faced discrimination.

trunk of the car of two African-American males who repeatedly came in contact with police engaged in the search for a serial sniper) was apparently compromised by the distraction of the assailants' race.

These are not the only available examples of such failures. Throughout the last century, reliance on racial profiling has repeatedly led to national security tragedies:

Japanese Internment During World War II

Signed by President [Franklin D.] Roosevelt in February 1942, Executive Order 9066 called for the removal of Japanese and Americans of Japanese ancestry from Western coastal regions to guarded internment camps. Located across the U.S., these permanent detention camps lasted until 1946, imprisoning over 110,000 people. Throughout the entire course of the war, 10 people were convicted of spying for Japan; none of them were of Japanese or even Asian descent.

The Oklahoma City Bombing

After bombing the Alfred P. Murrah federal building in Oklahoma City in April 1995, the white male assailant, Timothy McVeigh, was able to flee while law enforcement officers reportedly operated on the initial theory that "Arab terrorists" had committed the attack. . . .

Need to Learn from History

Fortunately, our nation's history also shows that law enforcement officials are capable of learning about the ineffectiveness of profiling based on inherent physical traits and changing their behavior accordingly. In the 1970s, the U.S. Secret Service relied upon a presidential assassin profile that said assailants would be males. After the arrest of Sara Jane Moore for taking a shot at President [Gerald] Ford, the gender limitation was removed from the profile. The value of changing the profile was verified in 1992 when a young woman was arrested for threatening to kill President George H.W. Bush after bringing a rifle to a rally where he was scheduled to speak.

However, the implications of this lesson seem to have been largely ignored with regard to race-based profiling. . . . Several of the United States' domestic "War on Terror" strategies (such as the post-9/11 attack roundups of Muslim and Arab men in New York City and the

Sara Jane Moore tried to assassinate President Gerald Ford in 1975. Her attempt motivated law enforcement to expand its profile of assassins to include women.

National Security Entry/Exit Registration Program) appear to have been conceived without appreciation for past mistakes. . . . While a wide range of "post–September 11, 2001," policies and practices seem to be informed by the fact that all of the 19 hijackers on the day of the attacks were Middle-Eastern males, U.S. law enforcement seems often to have acted in ways that ignore the facts that: (a) the overwhelming majority of people who belong to Arab-American, Muslim-American, and South-Asian-American communities are innocent and law abiding, and (b) many of the Al Qaeda sympathizers detained

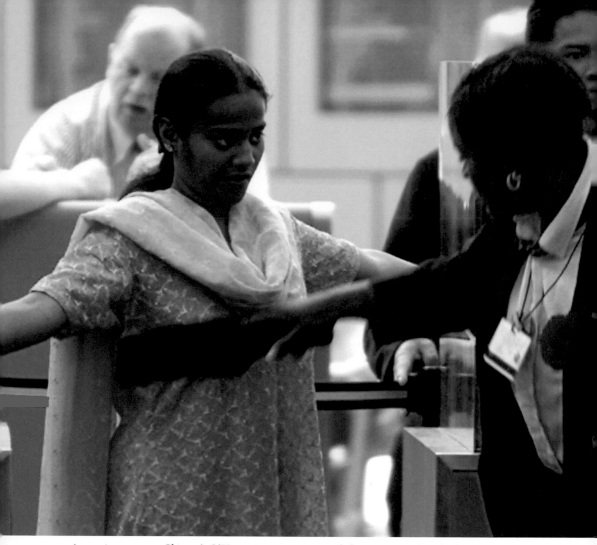

A security agent at Chicago's O'Hare airport uses a metal-detecting wand to check a passenger for concealed weapons or explosives.

since have come from a wide range of other ethnic groups and nationalities (such as Chicano American Jose Padilla, white American Taliban combatant John Walker Lindh, and the British "shoe-bomber" Richard Reid).

What is more, the decision to focus, even partially, on racial characteristics instead of on behaviors runs counter to a significant lesson learned from one of the most relevant changes in U.S. airport security policy in the last ten years. In the 1990s, spurred by discrimination lawsuits, the U.S. Customs Service eliminated the use of race in deciding which individuals to stop and search and instead began relying on a list of suspect behaviors. According to a study of U.S. Customs by Lamberth Consulting, the policy shift to color-blind profiling techniques increased the rate of productive searches—searches that led to discovery of illegal contraband or activity—by more than 300 percent.

If history is any judge, the impact of this failure to forgo the distraction of race-based strategies means that all Americans will continue to be at risk of attacks by individuals whose physical appearance or ethnicity defies popular stereotypes about terrorist conspirators. Meanwhile, law enforcement resources will continue to be squandered on over-scrutinizing millions of American citizens and visitors, ultimately because of how they look, where they or their ancestors are from, or what they wear.

EVALUATING THE AUTHORS' ARGUMENTS:

The authors in chapter 2 make different arguments about whether civil liberties should be restricted in order to effectively fight terrorism. If you were to write an essay on this topic, what would be your opinion? Does the threat of terrorism justify the curtailment of civil liberties? What evidence would you use to support your case?

CHAPTER 3

Are Civil Liberties in the United States Threatened?

Mohammad Aslam
Pervez
Pakistani
DISAPPEARED
in the USA

A Pakistani woman in New York demands an end to the practice of racial profiling.

The Patriot Act Threatens Civil Liberties

Nadine Strossen and Timothy H. Edgar

"[Patriot Act] powers make abuses far more likely because they remove the checks and balances that prevent abuse."

In the following viewpoint Nadine Strossen and Timothy H. Edgar assert that the Patriot Act is a threat to the civil liberties of Americans. The act undermines important checks and balances and gives the government new surveillance and detention powers and increased secrecy, argue Strossen and Edgar, making it easy to abuse the civil liberties of its citizens. In addition, say the authors, the government does not even need these increased powers in order to effectively fight terrorism. Strossen is president of the American Civil Liberties Union, an organization dedicated to protecting civil liberties in the United States. Edgar serves as legislative counsel for the organization.

AS YOU READ, CONSIDER THE FOLLOWING QUESTIONS:

1. What values have allowed the United States to grow abundantly, in the authors' opinion?
2. According to Strossen and Edgar, why is it difficult to get an accurate picture of Patriot Act abuses?
3. As argued by the authors, why is it a myth to say that without the Patriot Act, the government lacked adequate power to detain terrorist suspects?

Nadine Strossen and Timothy H. Edgar, testimony before the U.S. Senate Committee on the Judiciary, Washington, DC, November 18, 2003.

America faces a crucial test. That test is whether we—the political descendents of [former U.S. presidents Thomas] Jefferson and [James] Madison, and citizens of the world's oldest democracy—have the confidence, ingenuity and commitment to secure our safety without sacrificing our liberty.

For here we are at the beginning of the 21st century, in a battle with global terror. Terrorism is a new and different enemy. As a nation, we learned this on September 11, 2001, when a group of terrorists attacked us here at home, and within the space of minutes murdered nearly 3,000 of our fellow Americans and citizens of other nations, innocent civilians going about their everyday lives. . . .

Liberty Is Threatened

We must be ready to defend liberty, for liberty cannot defend itself. We as a nation have no trouble understanding the necessity of a military defense. But there is another equally powerful defense that is required, and that is the defense of our Constitution—the defense of our most cherished freedoms.

Put aside our popular culture which changes by the day, and our material success which is now vulnerable to the vicissitudes of the global economy—strip away all that is truly superficial. What is left that distinguishes us if not our constitutional values? These values—freedom, liberty, equality and tolerance—are the very source of our strength as a nation and the bulwark of our democracy. They are what have permitted us to grow abundantly, and to absorb wave after wave of immigrants to our shores, reaping the benefits of their industrious energy.

Now, we are in danger of allowing ourselves to be governed by our fears, rather than our values. How else can we explain the actions of our government over the last two years [since the September 11 attacks] to invade the privacy of our personal lives and to curtail immigrants' rights, all in the name of increasing our security? . . .

Excessive Power

Americans are concerned because the PATRIOT Act put in place statutory authority for the government to get a court order to come into your home without your knowledge and even take property without notifying you until weeks or months later. Americans are concerned because the PATRIOT Act allows the government to obtain many detailed, personal records—including library and bookstore records, financial and medical records, and Internet communications—without probable cause and without meaningful judicial review. For those records that may be obtained using "national security letters," there is no judicial review at all. Americans are concerned because the PATRIOT Act—as well as changes to immigration regulations since 9/11 and the President's claimed authority to detain "enemy

A woman in Boston protests the provisions of the Patriot Act.

The Patriot Act gives police a much wider range of power. Police are shown here confiscating property from a Detroit business suspected of having terrorist connections.

combatants"—all sanction indefinite detention without criminal charge and without meaningful judicial review.

Some have dismissed these concerns, saying the government has not used some of these anti-terrorism powers, or has used them appropriately. . . . Unfortunately, the Administration's excessive secrecy prevents the American people from getting an adequate picture about its use of PATRIOT Act surveillance powers.

What the ACLU [American Civil Liberties Union] can say for certain is that these and other powers make abuses far more likely because they remove the checks and balances that prevent abuse. Excessive power has, throughout our history, inevitably been used excessively. . . .

Destroying Checks and Balances

The government's new surveillance and detention powers have undermined important checks and balances, diminished personal privacy, increased government secrecy, and exacerbated inequality. . . .

The genius of our founding fathers was to design a system in which no one branch of government possessed all power, but instead the powers were divided among legislative, executive and judicial branches.

The government's actions since September 11 have undermined this system. Prior to September 11, the government had ample power to investigate, detain, convict and punish terrorists, with meaningful judicial review. The changes have made that review less meaningful.

Undermining Judicial Review

It is a myth to say that prior to September 11, the government could wiretap organized crime suspects but not terrorist suspects. In fact, the government has always had far greater powers to wiretap foreign terrorist suspects, because it could use either its criminal or its intelligence powers to do so. The PATRIOT Act simply enlarged further the already loose standards for both kinds of wiretapping.

FAST FACT

The Patriot Act allows federal agents to secretly search a citizen's home. In a 2004 Gallup poll, seven in ten people said they did not believe the government should have this power.

It is a myth to say that prior to September 11, the government was prevented by the Foreign Intelligence Surveillance Act from sharing information acquired in intelligence investigations with criminal prosecutors. In fact, it could do so, under procedures designed to ensure the intelligence powers were not being abused as a prosecutorial end-run around the Fourth Amendment. The

Source: Keefe. © 2003 by Cagle Cartoons, Inc. Reproduced by permission.

PATRIOT Act did not authorize such information sharing—it was already legal. Rather, the Act reduced the judicial oversight designed to prevent abuses of information sharing.

It is a myth that the government lacked adequate power to detain terrorist suspects. In fact, the government could, and did, detain many terrorist suspects prior to September 11 using both immigration and criminal powers. Indeed, President [George W.] Bush joined the ACLU in criticizing the use of secret evidence against some Arab and Muslim immigration detainees under the Clinton Administration. The PATRIOT Act, and government changes to detention regulations, did not authorize detention of terrorism suspects. Rather, it made immigration hearings and judicial review of those detentions far less meaningful.

It is a myth that the government could not effectively prosecute foreign terrorists without revealing classified information. The Classified Information Procedures Act has long been on the books to protect the government's secrets while ensuring a fair trial, and prosecutors of prior [terrorist group] Al Qaeda plots have said the Act worked well to protect both the rights of the accused and the national security of the government. . . .

It is a myth that the government could not listen to the conversations of attorneys who betrayed their profession by abusing the attorney-client privilege to implicate themselves in their clients' ongoing criminal acts. The government could always obtain a court order, based on probable cause, to listen in to conversations that lacked the protection of the attorney-client privilege. The monitoring regulation was drafted to evade that requirement of judicial oversight.

Understanding how these actions undermine checks and balances illustrates the sophistry of one of the government's main defenses of its post 9-11 actions. Government officials point out that courts have not struck down many of their actions—but their actions are a threat to liberty precisely because they are calculated to undermine the role of the courts, diminishing their oversight of government action.

EVALUATING THE AUTHORS' ARGUMENTS:

List the different arguments Nadine Strossen and Timothy H. Edgar use to support their contention that the Patriot Act threatens civil liberties. Rank them in order of most convincing to least convincing.

The Patriot Act Does Not Threaten Civil Liberties

"The [Patriot] Act uses court-tested safeguards . . . to aid the war against terrorism, while protecting the rights and lives of citizens."

John Ashcroft

John Ashcroft served as the U.S. attorney general from 2001 to 2005. In the following viewpoint, excerpted from a speech before the Federalist Society National Convention, Ashcroft argues that the Patriot Act gives the federal government critical tools for preventing terrorism in the United States. The act has allowed U.S. law enforcement and intelligence agencies to identify and disrupt numerous terrorist groups and plots to attack the United States, he maintains. At the same time, explains Ashcroft, the act safeguards civil liberties by preserving the system of checks and balances that exists between each branch of government.

AS YOU READ, CONSIDER THE FOLLOWING QUESTIONS:
1. What is "ordered liberty," as explained by Ashcroft?
2. In the author's opinion, how does the Constitution balance freedom and security?
3. According to Ashcroft, how has oversight of the executive branch been built in to the Patriot Act?

John Ashcroft, prepared remarks before the Federalist Society National Convention, November 15, 2003.

D ebate about how best to preserve and protect our liberty in the face of a very real terrorist threat [has been occurring since the September 11, 2001, terrorist attacks].

America has an honored tradition of debate and dissent under the First Amendment. It is an essential piece of our constitutional and cultural fabric. As a former politician, I have heard a few dissents in my time, and even expressed a couple of my own.

The Founders believed debate should enlighten, not just enliven. It should reveal truth, not obscure it. The future of freedom demands that our discourse be based on a solid foundation of facts and a sincere desire for truth. As we consider the direction and destiny of our nation, the friends of freedom must practice for themselves . . . and demand from others . . . a debate informed by fact and directed toward truth.

Take away all the bells and whistles . . . the rhetorical flourishes and occasional vitriol . . . and the current debate about liberty is about the rule of law and the role of law.

Ordered Liberty

The notion that the law can enhance, not diminish, freedom is an old one. [Philosopher] John Locke said the end of law is, quote, " . . . not to abolish or restrain but to preserve and enlarge freedom." [Former U.S. president] George Washington called this, "ordered liberty."

There are some voices in this discussion of how best to preserve freedom that reject the idea that law can enhance freedom. They think that passage and enforcement of any law is necessarily an infringement of liberty.

Ordered liberty is the reason that we are the most open and the most secure society in the world. Ordered liberty is a guiding principle, not a stumbling block to security.

When the first societies passed and enforced the first laws against murder, theft and rape, the men and women of those societies unquestionably were made more free.

A test of a law, then, is this: does it honor or degrade liberty? Does it enhance or diminish freedom?

The Founders provided the mechanism to protect our liberties and preserve the safety and security of the Republic: the Constitution. It is a document that safeguards security, but not at the expense of freedom.

It celebrates freedom, but not at the expense of security. It protects us *and* our way of life.

Since September 11, 2001, the Department of Justice has fought for, Congress has created, and the judiciary has upheld, legal tools that honor the Constitution . . . legal tools that are making America safer while enhancing American freedom.

It is a compliment to all who worked on the Patriot Act to say that it is not constitutionally innovative. The Act uses court-tested safeguards and time-honored ideas to aid the war against terrorism, while protecting the rights and lives of citizens.

[Former U.S. president James] Madison noted in 1792 that the greatest threat to our liberty was centralized power. Such focused power, he wrote, is liable to abuse. That is why he concluded a distribution of power into separate departments is a first principle of free governments.

FAST FACT

In a 2003 poll Fox News found that 55 percent of Americans believed the Patriot Act was a "good thing" for the country, with only 27 percent who said it was a "bad thing."

The Patriot Act honors Madison's "first principles" . . . giving each branch of government a role in ensuring both the lives and liberties of our citizens are protected. The Patriot Act grants the executive branch critical tools in the war on terrorism. It provides the legislative branch extensive oversight. It honors the judicial branch with court supervision over the Act's most important powers.

Executive Tools

First, the executive branch.

At the Department of Justice, we are dedicated to detecting, disrupting, and dismantling the networks of terror before they can strike at our nation. In the past two years [since September 11, 2001,] no major terrorist attack has been perpetrated on our soil. . . .

We are using the tough tools provided in the USA Patriot Act to defend American lives and liberty from those who have shed blood and decimated lives in other parts of the world.

The Patriot Act does three things:

First, it closes the gaping holes in law enforcement's ability to collect vital intelligence information on terrorist enterprises. It allows law enforcement to use proven tactics long used in the fight against organized crime and drug dealers.

Second, the Patriot Act updates our anti-terrorism laws to meet the challenges of new technology and new threats.

During his tenure as attorney general, John Ashcroft ardently endorsed the Patriot Act as an indispensable tool in the war on terrorism.

Third, with these critical new investigative tools provided by the Patriot Act, law enforcement can share information and cooperate better with each other. From prosecutors to intelligence agents, the Act allows law enforcement to "connect the dots" and uncover terrorist plots before they are launched. . . .

One thing the Patriot Act does not do is allow the investigation of individuals, quote, " . . . solely upon the basis of activities protected by the first amendment to the Constitution of the United States."

Even if the law did not prohibit it, the Justice Department has neither the time nor the inclination to delve into the reading habits or other First Amendment activities of our citizens. . . .

The Patriot Act was passed to give the CIA and other intelligence and law enforcement agencies the tools needed to prevent further terrorist attacks.

The Patriot Act has enabled us to make quiet, steady progress in the war on terror.

Since September 11, we have dismantled terrorist cells in Detroit, Seattle, Portland, Tampa, Northern Virginia, and Buffalo.

We have disrupted weapons procurement plots in Miami, San Diego, Newark, and Houston.

We have shut down terrorist-affiliated charities in Chicago, Dallas, and Syracuse. . . .

Terrorists who are incarcerated, deported or otherwise neutralized threaten fewer American lives. For two years, our citizens have been safe. There have been no major terrorist attacks on our soil. American freedom has been enhanced, not diminished. The Constitution has been honored, not degraded.

Legislative Oversight

Second, the role Congress plays.

In six weeks of debate in September and October of 2001, both the House of Representatives and the Senate examined studiously and debated vigorously the merits of the Patriot Act. In the end, both houses supported overwhelmingly its passage.

Congress built into the Patriot Act strict and structured oversight of the Executive Branch. Every six months, the Justice Department provides Congress with reports of its activities under the Patriot Act. . . .

Legislative oversight of the executive branch is critical to ordered liberty." It ensures that laws and those who administer them respect the rights and liberties of the citizens. . . .

Time and again, Congress has found the Patriot Act to be effective against terrorist threats, and respectful and protective of citizens' liberties. The Constitution has been honored, not degraded.

Judicial Supervision

Finally, the judiciary.

The Patriot Act provides for close judicial supervision of the executive branch's use of Patriot Act authorities.

The Act allows the government to utilize many long-standing, well-accepted law enforcement tools in the fight against terror. These tools

Congress (shown here in session) is charged with monitoring the actions of agencies empowered by the Patriot Act. To date, no abuses have been identified.

include delayed notification, judicially-supervised searches, and so-called roving wiretaps, which have long been used in combating organized crime and in the war on drugs.

In using these tactics to fight terrorism, the Patriot Act includes an *additional* layer of protection for individual liberty. A federal judge supervises the use of each of these tactics.

Were we to seek an order to request business records, that order would need the approval of a federal judge. Grand jury subpoenas issued for similar requests by police in standard criminal investigations are issued without judicial oversight.

Throughout the Patriot Act, tools provided to fight terrorism require that the same predication be established before a federal judge as with similar tools provided to fight other crime. . . .

The Power of Freedom

There is nothing more noble than fighting to preserve our God-given rights. Our proven tactics against the terrorist threat are helping to do just that.

[Since the September 11 terrorist attacks] we have protected the lives of our citizens here at home. Again and again, Congress has determined and the courts have determined that our citizens' rights have been respected. . . .

Terrorists attacked our nation thinking our liberties were our weakness.

They were wrong. The American people have fulfilled the destiny shaped by our forefathers and founders, and revealed the power of freedom.

Time and again, the spirit of our nation has been renewed and our greatness as a people has been strengthened by our dedication to the cause of liberty, the rule of law and the primacy and dignity of the individual.

I know we will keep alive these noble aspirations that lie in the hearts of all our fellow citizens, and for which our young men and women are at this moment fighting and making the ultimate sacrifice.

What we are defending is what generations before us fought for and defended: a nation that is a standard, a beacon, to all who desire a land that promises to uphold the best hopes of all mankind. A land of justice. A land of liberty.

EVALUATING THE AUTHORS' ARGUMENTS:

What type of evidence does John Ashcroft use to back up his assertion that the Patriot Act has been used to help prevent another terrorist attack on the United States? How do you think Nadine Strossen and Timothy H. Edgar might reply to Ashcroft's claim that U.S. law enforcement and intelligence agencies need the powers granted them under the act?

Immigrants Have Been Treated Unfairly in the War on Terrorism

Carol F. Khawly

"Discriminatory immigration regulations . . . [have] eroded civil rights and civil liberties for all."

Carol F. Khawly is a legal adviser for the American-Arab Anti-Discrimination Committee, a Washington, D.C.–based organization dedicated to protecting and promoting the rights of Arab Americans. In the following viewpoint she maintains that in its war against terrorism, the United States has treated Arab and Muslim immigrant communities unfairly, subjecting them to detention, special registration, and interviews. These discriminatory regulations do not make the United States safer from terrorism, argues Khawly, and they unfairly violate the civil liberties of immigrants.

AS YOU READ, CONSIDER THE FOLLOWING QUESTIONS:

1. In Khawly's opinion, why are many immigrants afraid to have a lawyer present when they are questioned?
2. What may happen to immigrants who fail to comply with special registration requirements, according to the author?
3. As explained by Khawly, why were many immigrants detained in Los Angeles, California?

Carol F. Khawly, testimony before the Congressional Asian Pacific American Caucus, November 4, 2003.

Following September 11, 2001, the government introduced a series of discriminatory immigration regulations and executive policies as part of a new national security campaign that has eroded civil rights and civil liberties for all. These measures, for the first time in many years, have amounted to the reintroduction of ethnic and national immigration discrimination into the American immigration system. Some of these policies include widespread operations of secret detentions, secret hearings and deportations, and "voluntary" interviews that have targeted the Arab and Muslim communities. The government has also renewed an immigration policy of special registration of aliens based on national origin and religion.

These government actions are reminiscent of an earlier era when thousands of Japanese Americans were interned and targeted in the name of national security during World War II simply because of their race/ethnicity. Just like the Japanese-American community, the Arab-American and Muslim communities have found themselves vulnerable to discrimination and racism based solely on race/ethnicity and religion. This selective enforcement and the climate it fostered have only served to create a culture of suspicion. Such government action has allowed, and in some instances encouraged, others to view the Arab-American community as suspect and disloyal.

FAST FACT

In the weeks after the September 11, 2001, terrorist attacks, more than one thousand immigrants, most of them Muslim, were arrested on suspicion of terrorism. Many were held for months, without charges.

"Voluntary" Interviews

In November 2001, the Department of Justice (DOJ) announced the first phase of a plan to interview and question 5000 foreign nationals who are young Arab men between the ages of 18 and 33. This program sent chills and panic through the community. ADC [American-Arab Anti-Discrimination Committee] received numerous calls from individuals stating that they were contacted by law enforcement and did not know why because they had not done anything wrong. Many explained that they were ready and willing to answer all questions, even

New York police stand guard in front of a mosque after the 9/11 attacks. Many Muslim Americans claim to be unfairly targeted by antiterrorism laws.

without an attorney because they were afraid that if they asserted their right to having a lawyer present, they might be perceived as being guilty or have something to hide.

In March 2002, the DOJ announced the second phase involving 3000 more interviewees. Another phase was announced with the start of the war on Iraq; this phase included the voluntary interviews of thousands of Iraqi Americans. Although the government insisted that the interviews were voluntary, many considered them compulsory. None of these interviews were based on any form of criminal or suspicious activity of the individual but rather on national origin and ethnicity. Some of the questions asked included information on one's immigration status, political affiliations and religious beliefs.

After the voluntary interviews, the DOJ also initiated a program to target 6000 Arab men out of 315,000 others who were wanted for deportation. The men were targeted because of national origin and religion. These types of selective enforcement measures continued to stigmatize our community.

Perhaps the most controversial and problematic program has been the Special Call-In Registration Program otherwise known as the National Security Entry-Exit Registration System (NSEERS).

NSEERS

The Department of Justice (DOJ) began implementing the National Security Entry-Exit Registration System (NSEERS) in September 2002. The program calls for the registration of foreign male nationals living in the US on temporary visas (tourist, business or student visas). Under the program, males 16 years or older from mostly Arab or Muslim countries are required to go to a designated immigration office to be interviewed, fingerprinted and photographed. . . . With the exception of North Korea, all countries designated under the program are Arab or Muslim. Group one includes Iran, Iraq, Libya, Sudan and Syria. Group two includes Afghanistan, Algeria, Bahrain, Eritrea, Lebanon, Morocco, Oman, Qatar, Somalia, Tunisia, United Arab Emirates, Yemen and North Korea. Group three includes Pakistan and Saudi Arabia, and Group four includes Bangladesh, Egypt, Indonesia, Jordan and Kuwait. . . .

Willful failure to comply with the special registration requirements is a crime and may result in arrest, fines, detention and/or deportation as well as denial of any future immigration benefits. Registrants must also submit to departure control requirements upon leaving the United States, that is, that the non-immigrant who is subject to special registration must be examined by an inspecting officer at the time of his or her departure, and to have his or her departure confirmed and recorded by the inspecting officer. Failure to fulfill the departure requirement will render the non-immigrant inadmissible in the future. Additionally, those who fail to register are entered into the NCIC database (FBI national criminal database) so that individuals can be

Arab American women demonstrate against post-9/11 legislation requiring certain immigrant groups to register with authorities.

identified, detained and deported in the course of routine traffic stops. . . .

While the Justice Department insists that this program is an anti-terrorism tool, the program is a failure in its foundation and does not assist in enhancing our national security. . . . This program unfortunately institutionalizes ethnic and gender discrimination. . . .

Unfair Treatment of Immigrants

The program's bias and inefficiency became most obvious with the aggressive implementation of the program in Los Angeles, California, when hundreds of individuals were rounded up as they came forward to voluntarily comply with the registration on the day of the first deadline for Group One. The INS [Immigration and Naturalization Service] office was completely unprepared to process the registrations.

Instead of extending the registration deadline or asking individuals to report back for registration, INS agents arrested and detained individuals so that it could later process their paperwork. Many of those arrested were held without bond. Others with pending adjustment applications, work authorization applications and other paperwork were also detained. . . .

Additionally, the program was used as a tool to detain and deport males who were on their way to obtaining legal status and who had no ties to terrorism. The program created widespread confusion, fear and anxiety in the Arab-American and Muslim communities. People who had lived in the US for years, had established family ties and jobs, but who had pending status applications (adjustment applications, labor certification applications, pending naturalization papers, etc.) were being detained and issued deportation orders. For example, a Sudanese national who had been granted "Temporary Protected Status" who went to the INS past the specified deadline was taken into custody. An Iranian-born naturalized Danish citizen whose mother is a US citizen and who has an approved petition for permanent residence was detained and denied bond. Although citizens, legal

Special registration requirements and the threat of deportation inspire fear in many law-abiding Muslim American families.

permanent residents ("green card holders"), asylum grantees, and diplomats are not required to register, in one instance, a US citizen from Lebanon and his wife who is a legal permanent resident were fingerprinted, interviewed and photographed at the Texas border upon their return from a vacation. . . .

An Unsound Strategy

Most importantly, however, and from a national security perspective, the program does not make us safer. Instead of finding terrorists, the program targets people based on national origin and religion rather than targeting behavior patterns and intelligence information. The government would have the public believe that the program identifies terrorists and is necessary for national security. This argument is illusory, because it assumes that the next threat will come from those countries. It also mistakenly assumes that a terrorist will come forward and register. The program is also being used as a vehicle to detain large numbers of individuals with no evidence that they pose a threat to national security.

EVALUATING THE AUTHORS' ARGUMENTS:

The author of this viewpoint and the author of the next viewpoint disagree over whether or not the civil liberties of U.S. immigrants have been harmed in the war on terrorism. Which author offers a more persuasive argument? Why?

Immigrants Have Been Treated Fairly in the War on Terrorism

"The detentions, the targeted interviews, and the other aggressive investigative techniques we are currently employing are all legal under the Constitution."

Michael Chertoff

In the following viewpoint Michael Chertoff argues that the constitutional rights of immigrants have been upheld in America's war on terrorism. Aggressive measures such as detentions and questioning of immigrants have been used, says Chertoff, but these are necessary to combat the unique and challenging threat posed by the al Qaeda terrorist group. He maintains that all treatment of U.S. immigrants are completely legal according to the country's Constitution. Chertoff is the U.S. assistant attorney general, in charge of the Justice Department's Criminal Division.

AS YOU READ, CONSIDER THE FOLLOWING QUESTIONS:
1. According to Chertoff, what is the intent of Osama bin Laden and al Qaeda members regarding Americans?
2. What are "sleepers," as explained by the author?
3. In Chertoff's opinion, what is the best way to combat sleepers and other terrorist threats?

Michael Chertoff, testimony before the U.S. Senate Committee on the Judiciary, Washington, DC, November 28, 2001.

The country faces a truly extraordinary threat to our national security and the physical safety of the American people. . . . [The] prevention of future terrorist attacks [has become] our top and overriding priority. We are pursuing that priority aggressively and systematically with a national and international investigation of unprecedented scope, but we are carefully doing so within established constitutional and legal limits. . . .

Committed to Killing Americans

I would like to briefly outline the nature of the threat we are facing and explain why we believe the threat necessitates the type of investigative response we have been pursuing. . . .

The overwhelming, brute fact of [the] September 11th [2001, attacks] is this: This country was wantonly and deceitfully assaulted by an enemy intent on destroying as many innocent lives as possible. Before September 11th, [terrorist leader] Usama Bin Laden and his henchmen wanted to kill thousands of innocent American civilians. On September 11th, they succeeded. Since September 11th, Bin Laden and his co-conspirators have brazenly announced that they will kill more of us. He and his followers actually believe they have a duty to kill Americans. And those are not my words; those are his words.

In a February 1998 directive, Bin Laden ordered his followers "to kill Americans and plunder their money whenever and wherever they find it." [In October 2001] Bin Laden made a video declaring to his supporters in the Al Qaida [terrorist group] network: "Bush and Blair . . . don't understand any language but the language of force. Every time they kill us, we will kill them, so the balance of terror can be achieved." He went on: "The battle has been moved inside America, and we shall continue until we win this battle, or die in the cause and meet our maker."

A Challenging Enemy

So we have a terrorist organization with thousands of members and followers worldwide, which is fanatically committed to killing Americans on our own soil, through suicide attacks if necessary. And unlike the enemies we have faced in past wars, this is an enemy that comes not openly, but cravenly, in disguise. We know from what we

A rescue worker rests during cleanup efforts after the 9/11 attacks. In the wake of the attacks, the government began working to ensure a tragedy of such magnitude would never occur again.

have learned about the 19 hijackers from September 11th and what we know about those responsible for earlier attacks against America that the terrorists in the Al Qaida network plan their terror years in advance. They are sophisticated, meticulous, and very patient.

Of particular concern is their use of so-called "sleepers." A sleeper is a committed terrorist sent sometimes years in advance into a possible target location, where he may assume a new identity and lead an outwardly normal lifestyle, while waiting to spring into action to conduct or assist in a terrorist attack. . . . I can give you an illustrative example of a sleeper from one of the 1998 embassy bombing cases.

Al Qaida member Mohamed Sadeek Odeh (inset) was convicted in 2001 for participating in the August 1998 bombing of the U.S. embassy in Nairobi, Kenya.

Mohamed Sadeek Odeh was convicted early [in 2001] for participating in the August 1998 bombing of the U.S. embassy in Nairobi,
Kenya. . . .

Odeh became a sworn member of Al Qaida in 1992 in Afghanistan
and was subsequently sent to Somalia to train Islamic militants.
In 1994, Odeh moved to Mombasa, a coastal town in southeast
Kenya. . . .

After living in Mombasa for a few years, Odeh moved to Malindi,
another coastal town in Kenya, and then later to a small village known
as Witu, where he lived until August 1998. At all times, Odeh lived
modestly and quietly. For example, in Witu, Odeh lived in a hut,
where he had no telephone or other means of communication.

But when the time came to participate in plotting the embassy
bombings, Odeh sprang into action. In the Spring and Summer
of 1998, he met other Al Qaida members in Kenya and discussed
ways to attack the United States. In the days immediately preced-
ing the August 7, 1998, embassy bombings, Odeh met repeatedly
with Al Qaida members who participated in the bombing in
Mombasa and Nairobi. Hours before the bombing, Odeh suddenly left Kenya, flying to Pakistan during the night of August 6 and
through to the early morning of August 7. Odeh was detained at
the Karachi airport (due to a bad false passport), and eventually
returned to Kenya.

Odeh is just one example of how an Al Qaida member was able
over time to integrate himself into the local environment in a way
that made his terrorist activities much more difficult to detect. . . .

The Necessity of Aggressive Measures

How can we combat the terrorists' use of sleepers? In many ways it is
more difficult than trying to find a needle in a haystack because here
the needle is masquerading as a stalk of hay. We could continue as
before, and hope we get lucky. . . . Or, as we are currently doing, we
can pursue a comprehensive and systematic investigative approach,
informed by all-source intelligence, that aggressively uses every available legally permissible investigative technique to try to identify, disrupt and, if possible, incarcerate or deport sleepers and other persons
who pose possible threats to our national security.

Are Immigration Restrictions Necessary?

Two 2002 polls found that most voters favor making it more difficult for all foreigners to enter the United States.

Question:
Do you favor or oppose making it more difficult for all foreigners, regardless of country, to enter the United States?

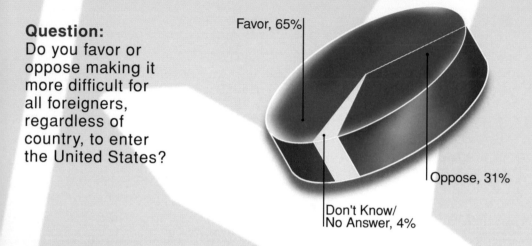

Favor, 65%

Oppose, 31%

Don't Know/
No Answer, 4%

Question:
Which comes closest to your view about the number of immigrants from Muslim countries that should be allowed into the United States?

A) The United States should not allow any immigrants from Muslim countries.

B) The United States should reduce the number of immigrants from Muslim countries.

C) The United States should continue to allow the same number of immigrants from Muslim countries as now.

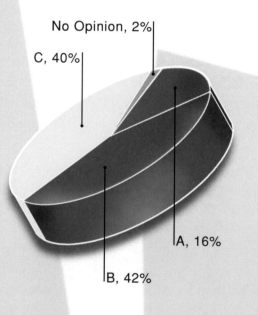

No Opinion, 2%

C, 40%

A, 16%

B, 42%

Sources: Quinnipiac University, 2002; Gallup Organization, 2002.

Without understanding the challenge we face, one cannot understand the need for the measures we have employed. Are we being aggressive and hard-nosed? You bet. In the aftermath of September 11th, how could we not be? Our fundamental duty to protect America and its people requires no less.

Yet it is equally important to emphasize that the detentions, the targeted interviews, and the other aggressive investigative techniques we are currently employing are all legal under the Constitution and applicable federal law as it existed both before and after September 10th. . . . As federal prosecutors, we have great discretion under the Constitution and well-established federal law to decide how aggressively to investigate and charge cases. In light of the extraordinary threat facing our country, we have made a decision to exercise our lawful prosecutorial discretion in a way that we believe maximizes our chances of preventing future attacks against America.

EVALUATING THE AUTHOR'S ARGUMENTS:

What evidence does Michael Chertoff give to support his argument that immigrants in the United States have been treated fairly following the September 11, 2001, terrorist attacks? Do you believe his evidence is sufficient to prove his case? Explain your answer.

VIEWPOINT

5

Media Censorship Endangers Civil Liberties

Sean Turner

"What is truly 'indecent' or 'improper' is the mere existence of a [media] regulatory entity."

The Federal Communications Commission (FCC) is the federal agency that regulates broadcast media in the United States. In the following viewpoint Sean Turner asserts that the scope of this regulation is continually increasing and is a serious threat to civil liberties. Individuals have the ability to control their own media exposure, argues Turner. In his opinion, government regulation means that the government is imposing its own perception of morality on the public, and this is an unconstitutional assault on free speech. Turner is a regular columnist for GOPUSA.com, RenewAmerica.us, and MensNews Daily.com, and a contributor to a number of news and political Web sites.

AS YOU READ, CONSIDER THE FOLLOWING QUESTIONS:
1. How did 1927 "usher in the first phase of censorship" according to Turner?
2. What does the FCC regulate, as explained by the author?
3. In Turner's opinion, what is the best way to protect children from being exposed to media indecency?

Sean Turner, "FCC—Federal Censorship Commission," www.renewamerica.us, June 15, 2004. Copyright © 2004 by Sean Turner. Reproduced by permission.

The recent record-setting $2 million settlement between Clear Channel Communications Inc. and the FCC [Federal Communications Commission] should come as no surprise to those cognizant of the increasing regulatory grip of the federal government over the affairs of the businesses and citizens within its purview.[1] What is surprising—well, actually disturbing—is the multitude of people who would agree with such a settlement and the charges that led to it. At issue were on-air remarks made earlier this year by [radio personality] Howard Stern—deemed "indecent" by both Clear Channel Communications and the federal government. What is truly "indecent" or "improper" is the mere existence of a regulatory entity—the FCC—that seeks and succeeds in dictating the content of broadcast communications. A brief look into the history of the FCC reveals the transformation from merely a communications gatekeeper—bad—to today's content czar—worse.

Ushering in Censorship

The year 1927 was filled with a number of events that would leave an indelible mark on the lives of millions in America, and around the world. It was a year that witnessed the birth of [actor] Sidney Poitier and [jazz musician] Stan Getz, the destruction of the "Great Mississippi Flood," the opening of the Holland Tunnel [connecting Manhattan and New Jersey] and the first transatlantic telephone call (from New York to London). It was also the year, in which the Radio Act of 1927 became law—which laid the groundwork for today's Federal Communications Commission. Ratified by President Calvin Coolidge— a Republican whose inauguration was the first presidential inauguration broadcast on radio—the Radio Act of 1927 led to the formation of the Federal Radio Commission, which was created to license broadcasters

FAST FACT

According to the Center for Public Integrity, in 2004 the FCC collected $3.66 million in fines for indecency.

---

1. In 2004 the FCC imposed numerous fines on Clear Channel for indecency. Clear Channel paid an almost $2 million settlement that cleared it of all charges of indecency.

and ostensibly reduce radio interference. This legislation superseded the Radio Act of 1912—giving regulatory authority over radio communication to the Department of Commerce and the Interstate Commerce Commission—and ushered in the first phase of censorship by prohibiting the utterance of any "obscene, indecent, or profane language by means of radio communication."

In 1934, FDR [former U.S. president Franklin Delano Roosevelt] and Congress continued its assault on free speech and growth of regulatory constraints through the Communications Act of 1934—which replaced the Federal Radio Commission with the Federal Communications Commission (FCC). Though the act remains the foundation of the regulatory authority of the FCC, it has undergone a number of amendments—most notable among these is what led to the creation of "public" television, and the Cable Act of 1984.

The Federal Communications Commission regulates the content of all stations broadcasting over public airwaves, including this small AM station in New York.

In a 2004 poll of 1,000 people, the majority of respondents believed that parents, not government, should be responsible for keeping inappropriate material away from children.

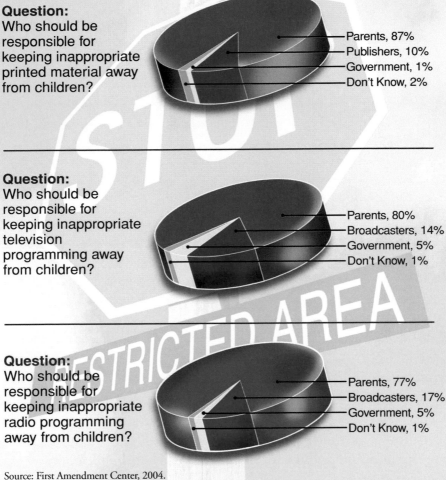

Question:
Who should be responsible for keeping inappropriate printed material away from children?

- Parents, 87%
- Publishers, 10%
- Government, 1%
- Don't Know, 2%

Question:
Who should be responsible for keeping inappropriate television programming away from children?

- Parents, 80%
- Broadcasters, 14%
- Government, 5%
- Don't Know, 1%

Question:
Who should be responsible for keeping inappropriate radio programming away from children?

- Parents, 77%
- Broadcasters, 17%
- Government, 5%
- Don't Know, 1%

Source: First Amendment Center, 2004.

Continual Attempts to Restrict Free Speech

As new communications technologies emerged, so too did efforts by Congress to restrict content and increase the FCC hegemony over communication in America. One such example is the Communications Decency Act, which criminalized the use of computers to display "indecent" material, unless the content provider "effective" method

U.S. senators review a television program during a 1997 hearing on decency in broadcasting. Many Americans condemn regulation of the media as a form of censorship.

is used to prohibit access to that material to anyone under the age of 18. Although this and portions of the act were invalidated by the Supreme Court in 1997 as a violation of the First Amendment, efforts have continued by Congress and state legislatures over the years to restrict Internet content—among other media.

The FCC regulates all non–Federal Government use of the radio spectrum—which includes radio and television broadcasting, all inter-state telecommunications, and all international communications whose origin or destination is the United States. Its primary method of enforcement was once merely the revocation of licenses, as fines were apparently an ineffective method of censorship. However, and per-haps sensing the impending litigation, the FCC, with the continual assistance from Congress, is placing less emphasis on license revoca-tion, and is seeking to increase maximum fines into the hundreds of thousands of dollars per utterance anything deemed "indecent." And since the Supreme Court has already ruled that the FCC has the authority to place some restrictions on content, don't expect any successful attempts to cut off any of the FCC's regulatory appendages any time soon.

Not the Government's Responsibility

So there you have it . . . another chapter, decades in the making, of the incessant reduction of freedom. As usual, free speech has taken a back seat to the often well-intentioned, but usually misguided attempts to impose a perception of morality on the public. Given the widespread support that these attempts have enjoyed, it is apparent that good parenting and monitoring one's own children are tasks best left to government. I guess it is too burdensome for a parent nowadays to monitor what their child listens to or watches. Moreover, it seems there are quite a few who are unable to locate the television, radio, or computer's off button. When many such individuals or groups fail to accomplish their agenda on their own—they simply run to mommy and daddy government to make it all better.

EVALUATING THE AUTHORS' ARGUMENTS:

Sean Turner, the author of this viewpoint, and L. Brent Bozell III, the author of the next viewpoint, disagree strongly on FCC regulation of media content. After reading these viewpoints, can you think of any points these authors might agree on regarding media censorship? Explain.

VIEWPOINT 6

Media Censorship Does Not Endanger Civil Liberties

L. Brent Bozell III

L. Brent Bozell III is the founder and president of the Parents Television Council, an organization dedicated to ensuring that children are not exposed to sex, violence, and profanity on television and in other media. In the following viewpoint he argues that the majority of people do not want to see or hear indecent content in the media. While free speech includes the right to say offensive things, it also includes the right to protest offensive speech, says Bozell. Thus, he concludes, media regulation by the Federal Communications Commission—the federal agency that regulates broadcast media—is not a violation of free speech because it merely reflects the opinions of the majority of Americans.

"Most people . . . like the idea that the FCC actually uphold the broadcast-obscenity laws."

AS YOU READ, CONSIDER THE FOLLOWING QUESTIONS:
1. As argued by the author, what happens when the work of radio shock jocks is actually held up to public scrutiny?
2. According to Bozell, why are censorship complaints hypocritical?
3. In the author's opinion, what do the media often censor when they discuss the topic of censorship?

L. Brent Bozell III, "Censorship—or Democracy?" www.parentstv.org, March 17, 2004. Copyright © 2004 by the Parents Television Council. Reproduced by permission.

I n the surging surf of the trashy tidal wave known as the Super
Bowl Halftime Show [in which singer Janet Jackson exposed her
breast], radio shock jocks are a very unhappy lot. Whether it's
Howard Stern or Don and Mike, the airwaves today are filled with
whining and complaining about the newly restrictive atmosphere ema-
nating from the Washington offices of the Federal Communications
Commission [FCC] and Congress.

The shock jocks make it sound like we've entered a Brave New World[1]
of autocratic censorship. The House has passed legislation by a resound-
ing 391-22 margin that would, among other things, increase fines
almost twenty-fold, to $500,000 with license-revocation hearings after
three offenses. The FCC for its part has stated it intends to get very
serious about curbing the abuses on the airwaves. In short, the old
formula—look for the next bound-
ary of taste to bowl over—doesn't
look like such a smart play right
now.

Opponents of the new trend
cry repression, censorship, the
repeal of the First Amendment.
But is the new trend censorship—
or democracy?

The Opinion
of the Majority

Ten years ago, the debate raged over
offensive images of "Piss Christ" and
Robert Mapplethorpe's sexualized
photos of naked young children, subsidized by every American taxpayer
through the National Endowment
for the Arts.[2] NEA lovers cried cen-
sorship. But by funding offensive "art" without consulting the taxpay-
ers, the real government-dictated or government-favored speech came

> # FAST FACT
>
> An estimated 6.6 million
> kids, ages two to eleven,
> were watching the 2004
> Super Bowl halftime show
> when Justin Timberlake
> ripped off a piece of Janet
> Jackson's bodice, exposing
> her right breast to the
> nationwide audience.
> Another 7.3 million teens
> ages twelve to seventeen
> were tuned in at that
> time.

---

1. *Brave New World* is a 1932 novel about a society that uses mind control to rule its population. 2. The NEA is
a federally funded program that offers funding and support for artists. In the early 1990s, it was criticized for
funding art that many people considered offensive.

from the NEA's cultural commissars, not the protesters. If the American people were allowed to vote on whether they would spend their pennies on "Piss Christ," the vast majority would veto that ridiculous expenditure.

Broadcast speech is not subsidized in the same way as NEA art—although the regulatory rationale for the FCC is based on the principle that the airwaves belong to the public. Radio and TV stations merely make a mint off them. The political problem for shock jocks is that when their "finest" work is held up to public scrutiny, most people can't believe they actually say and do these incredibly perverted things. They like the idea that the FCC actually uphold the broadcast-obscenity laws that have long been on the books.

Radio shock jock Howard Stern has been a frequent target of the Federal Communications Commission.

Although South Park, *a popular late-night cartoon, contains offensive material, its time slot caters to a mature audience.*

The Super Bowl sleazefest taught Washington and Los Angeles that when the most debased programming narrowcasted in the neatly compartmentalized youth culture—MTV [Music Television], Howard Stern, [television show] "South Park," you name it—is exposed to the broad mass of the American people, they go from passively unaware to actively outraged. Entertainment barons only care about the wallets of the young adults who show up in the ratings counts. Activists concerned about the degradation of the broader culture have gone to Washington demanding action to protect the airwaves they—and not [media company] Viacom—own.

Free Speech, Not Censorship

It's not censorship, it's democracy. It's community activism, free speech rising up to combat other free speech. Should a station be fined, and

Source: Wright. © by Tribune Media Services, Inc. All rights reserved. Reproduced by permission.

maybe even lose its license for repeated violations? Yes. If that's the only way to get the media giants to behave, so be it.

There's also a dollop of hypocrisy in the "censorship" complaints. When the offensive content is political instead of sexual—remember the infamous incident when the D.C. shock jock "The Greaseman" said black singer Lauryn Hill was so bad he could see why blacks get dragged behind trucks?—nobody warns of "censorship" or lectures about the First Amendment. They pack the shock jock's bags.

The hypocrisy doesn't end there, either. When the news media confronts the topic of broadcast indecency, they are quick to give credibility to the "censorship" argument, but then censor out the very content that's under discussion. News reports on Clear Channel sacking the Florida shock jock "Bubba the Love Sponge" after a $755,000 fine didn't often explain the kind of skits "Bubba" did.

In one skit, using cartoon music, he imagined favorite kiddie cartoon characters in sexual situations, with cartoon theme songs in the background. Shaggy was hooked on crack, so Scooby-Doo told him he could perform oral sex acts to pay for the drugs. George

Jetson tells his wife Jane he doesn't need Viagra because he's got a "Spacely Sprocket (bleep) ring," which then malfunctions. Alvin the Chipmunk complains he hasn't had sex in six weeks. . . .

How many parents would vote to have their children vulnerable to this garbage on the public airwaves daily? You can whine until the cows come home, Howard Stern. The public is fed up with you and your lot.

EVALUATING THE AUTHORS' ARGUMENTS:

Three of the authors in chapter 3 claim that civil liberties in the United States are threatened, while the other three contend that this is not the case. If you were to write an essay on the state of civil liberties in the United States, what would be your opinion? What evidence would you use to support your case?

FACTS ABOUT CIVIL LIBERTIES

Editor's Note: These facts can be used in reports or papers to rein-force or add credibility when making important points or claims.

Civil liberties are protections from the power of governments. Many coun-tries have constitutions that protect civil liberties.

Civil liberties in the United States are protected by the Constitution, espe-cially its Bill of Rights.

Some of the Rights Specifically Mentioned in the Body of the U.S. Constitution Are:

- writ of habeas corpus, a court order requiring government officials to present a prisoner in court and to explain to the judge why the person is being held
- no bills of attainder (legislative acts that punish an individual or group without judicial trial)
- trial by jury in federal courts
- limits on punishment for the crime of treason

Some of the Rights Specifically Mentioned in the Bill of Rights Are:

- The First Amendment guarantees freedom of speech, press, assem-bly, and petition. In addition, it prohibits Congress from establish-ing a national religion.
- The Second Amendment allows the right to bear arms.
- The Fourth Amendment restricts searches and seizures.
- The Fifth Amendment provides for grand juries, restricts eminent domain (the right of the government to take private property for public use), and prohibits forced self-incrimination and double jeop-ardy (being tried twice for the same crime).
- Amendment Six outlines criminal court procedures.
- Amendment Seven guarantees trial by jury in civil cases that involve values as low as twenty dollars.

- Amendment Eight prevents excessive bail and unusual punishment.

The Constitution of Canada includes the Canadian Charter of Rights and Freedoms, which protects many of the same rights as the U.S. Constitution.

The European Convention on Human Rights, signed by the United Kingdom and many European nations, protects civil liberties in those countries.

Historical Threats to Civil Liberties in the United States:

- 1798. In anticipation of war with France, the Alien Enemy Act authorizes the deportation of "alien enemy males 14 years and upwards."
- 1861. President Abraham Lincoln suspends the writ of habeas corpus in Pennsylvania, Delaware, Maryland, and the District of Columbia. The suspension is extended to all other states in 1863.
- 1918. The Entry and Departure Controls Act allows the president to control the departure and entry in times of war or national emergency of any noncitizen "whose presence was deemed contrary to public safety." The act is extended in 1941.
- 1942. President Franklin D. Roosevelt signs Executive Order 9066, banning all persons "deemed necessary or desirable" from "military areas." The act forces the relocation of more than one hundred thousand Japanese Americans to internment camps.
- 1950. The Internal Security Act makes it illegal for a member of a Communist organization to hold any nonelective office or employment in the United States, to be employed in a defense facility, or to apply for, or use, a passport.
- 1978. The Foreign Intelligence Surveillance Act is passed in response to increased terrorist activity around the world. The act authorizes electronic eavesdropping and wiretapping in the collection of foreign intelligence information. In 1994 it is expanded to permit covert physical searches.
- 1996. The Antiterrorism and Effective Death Penalty Act establishes membership in a terrorist organization as a ground for denying a noncitizen entry into the United States. The act also authorizes

officials to use court-ordered wiretapping to investigate various immigration offenses.

- 2001. The USA Patriot Act is enacted in response to the September 11, 2001, terrorist attacks. The act allows for indefinite detention of noncitizens, minimizes judicial supervision of surveillance by law enforcement authorities, and expands the ability of the government to conduct secret searches.

The September 11, 2001, Terrorist Attacks Impacted the Civil Liberties of Arab Americans:

- Soon after the attacks, the U.S. government began detaining people who fit the profile of the suspected hijackers: mostly male, Arabic, or Muslim noncitizens. By late November, more than twelve hundred people had been detained and held incommunicado.
- Immediately following the attacks, a Gallup poll found that 60 percent of Americans wanted Arabs to undergo more intensive screening at airports.
- In an October 2001 poll of Arab Americans, 20 percent said their civil liberties had been violated since the September 11 attacks, and 45 percent said they knew another Arab American who had faced a violation of civil liberties.

The First Amendment Center Conducts Yearly, Nationwide Surveys of Attitudes Toward the First Amendment in the United States. In 2004 the Organization Found That:

- Sixty-five percent of respondents indicated overall support for First Amendment freedoms, while 30 percent said the First Amendment goes too far.
- Fifty percent said they believe Americans have too little access to information about the federal government's efforts to combat terrorism—up from 40 percent in 2002.
- Just 28 percent rated America's education system as doing an "excellent" or "good" job of teaching students about First Amendment freedoms.

ORGANIZATIONS TO CONTACT

The editors have compiled the following list of organizations concerned with the issues debated in this book. The descriptions are derived from materials provided by the organizations. All have publications or information available for interested readers. The list was compiled on the day of publication of the present volume; names, addresses, phone and fax numbers, and e-mail and Internet addresses may change. Be aware that many organizations take several weeks or longer to respond to inquiries, so allow as much time as possible.

American Civil Liberties Union (ACLU)
125 Broad St., 18th Floor, New York, NY 10004
(212) 549-2500
fax: (212) 549-2646
e-mail: aclu@aclu.org
Web site: www.aclu.org

The ACLU is a national organization that defends Americans' civil liberties guaranteed in the U.S. Constitution. It adamantly opposes regulation of all forms of speech, including pornography and hate speech. The ACLU offers numerous reports, fact sheets, and policy statements on a wide variety of issues. Publications include the briefing papers "Freedom of Expression," "Hate Speech on Campus," and "Popular Music Under Siege."

American Library Association (ALA)
50 E. Huron St., Chicago, IL 60611
(800) 545-2433
fax: (312) 440-9347
e-mail: ala@ala.org
Web site: www.ala.org

The ALA is the nation's primary professional organization for librarians. Through its Office for Intellectual Freedom (OIF), the ALA supports free access to libraries and library materials. The OIF also monitors and opposes efforts to ban books. The ALA's sister organization, the Freedom to Read Foundation, provides legal defense for libraries. Publications of the ALA include the *Newsletter on Intellectual Freedom*, articles, fact sheets, and policy statements, including "Protecting the Freedom to Read."

Arab American Institute (AAI)

1600 K St. NW, Suite 601, Washington, DC 20006
(202) 429-9210
Web site: www.aaiusa.org

AAI is a nonprofit organization committed to the civic and political empowerment of Americans of Arab descent. The institute opposes ethnic profiling and the restriction of immigrants' civil liberties in the name of homeland security. It provides policy, research, and public affairs services to support a broad range of community activities. It publishes a quarterly newsletter called *Issues*, a weekly bulletin called *Countdown*, and the report *Healing the Nation: The Arab American Experience After September 11.*

Canadian Association for Free Expression (CAFE)

PO Box 332, Station B, Etobicoke, ON M9W 5L3 Canada
(905) 897-7221
e-mail: cafe@canadafirst.net
Web site: www.canadianfreespeech.com

CAFE, one of Canada's leading civil liberties groups, works to strengthen the freedom of speech and freedom of expression provisions in the Canadian Charter of Rights and Freedoms. It lobbies politicians and researches threats to freedom of speech. Publications include specialized reports, leaflets, and the *Free Speech Monitor*, which is published ten times per year.

Cato Institute

1000 Massachusetts Ave. NW, Washington, DC 20001
(202) 842-0200
fax: (202) 842-3490
e-mail: cato@cato.org
Web site: www.cato.org

The Cato Institute is a libertarian public policy research foundation dedicated to limiting the role of government and promoting individual liberty. The institute publishes the quarterly magazine *Regulation*, the bimonthly *Cato Policy Report*, and numerous papers dealing with civil liberties, including "Sex, Cyberspace, and the First Amendment," and "Titillating TV and Creeping Censorship."

Center for Constitutional Rights (CCR)
666 Broadway, 7th Floor, New York, NY 10012
(212) 614-6464
fax: (212) 614-6499
Web site: www.ccr-ny.org

CCR is a nonprofit legal and educational organization dedicated to protecting and advancing the rights guaranteed by the U.S. Constitution and the Universal Declaration of Human Rights. The organization uses litigation to empower minority and poor communities and to strengthen the broader movement for constitutional and human rights. It opposes the government's restriction of civil liberties since the September 11, 2001, terrorist attacks. CCR publishes books, pamphlets, fact sheets, and reports, such as *The State of Civil Liberties: One Year Later.*

Concerned Women for America (CWA)
1015 Fifteenth St. NW, Suite 110, Washington, DC 20005
(202) 488-7000
fax: (202) 488-0806
Web site: www.cwfa.org

CWA is a membership organization that promotes conservative values and is concerned with creating an environment that is conducive to building strong families and raising healthy children. CWA publishes the monthly *Family Voice*, which argues against all forms of pornography.

Electronic Frontier Foundation (EFF)
1550 Bryant St., Suite 725, San Francisco, CA 94103
(415) 436-9333
fax: (415) 436-9993
e-mail: ask@eff.org
Web site: www.eff.org

EFF is a nonprofit, nonpartisan organization that works to protect privacy and freedom of expression in the arena of computers and the Internet. Its missions include supporting litigation that protects First Amendment rights. EFF's Web site publishes an electronic bulletin, *Effector*, and the guidebook *Protecting Yourself Online: The Definitive Resource on Safety, Freedom, and Privacy in Cyberspace.*

Family Research Council (FRC)
700 Thirteenth St. NW, Suite 500, Washington, DC 20005
(202) 393-2100
fax: (202) 393-2134
e-mail: corrdept@frc.org
Web site: www.frc.org

The Family Research Council is an organization that believes pornography degrades women and children and seeks to strengthen current obscenity laws. It publishes the monthly newsletter *Washington Watch* and the bimonthly journal *Family Policy*, which features a full-length essay in each issue, such as "Keeping Libraries User and Family Friendly: The Challenge of Internet Pornography." The FRC also publishes policy papers, including "Indecent Proposal: The NEA Since the Supreme Court Decency Decision," and "Internet Filtering and Blocking Technology."

Freedom Forum
1101 Wilson Blvd., Arlington, VA 22209
(703) 528-0800
fax: (703) 284-2836
e-mail: news@freedomforum.org
Web site: www.freedomforum.org

The Freedom Forum is an international organization that works to protect freedom of the press and free speech. It monitors developments in media and First Amendment issues on its Web site, in its monthly magazine *Forum News*, and in the *Media Studies Journal*, published twice a year.

Free Speech Coalition
PO Box 10480, Canoga Park, CA 91309
(800) 845-8503
(818) 348-9373

e-mail: freespeech@pacificnet.net
Web site: www.freespeechcoalition.com

The Free Speech Coalition is a trade association that represents members of the adult entertainment industry. It seeks to protect the industry from attempts to censor pornography. Publications include the report *The Truth About the Adult Entertainment Industry.*

International Freedom of Expression Exchange (IFEX)
IFEX Clearing House, 489 College St., Suite 403
Toronto, ON M6G 1A5 Canada
(416) 515-9622
fax: (416) 515-7879
e-mail: ifex@ifex.org
Web site: www.ifex.org

IFEX consists of more than forty organizations that support freedom of expression. Its work is coordinated by the Toronto-based Clearing House. Through the Action Alert Network, organizations report abuses of free expression to the Clearing House, which distributes the information throughout the world. Publications include the weekly *Communiqué,* which reports on free expression triumphs and violations.

Morality in Media (MIM)
475 Riverside Dr., Suite 239, New York, NY 10115
(212) 870-3222
fax: (212) 870-2765
e-mail: mim@moralitymedia.org
Web site: www.moralitymedia.org

Morality in Media is an interfaith organization that fights obscenity and opposes indecency in the mainstream media. It believes pornography harms society and maintains the National Obscenity Law Center, a clearinghouse of materials on obscenity law. Publications include the bimonthlies *Morality in Media and Obscenity Law Bulletin,* and reports, including "Pornography's Effects on Adults and Children."

National Coalition Against Censorship (NCAC)
275 Seventh Ave., New York, NY 10001
(212) 807-6222

fax: (212) 807-6245
e-mail: ncac@ncac.org
Web site: www.ncac.org

The NCAC represents more than forty national organizations that work to prevent suppression of free speech and the press. It educates the public about the dangers of censorship and how to oppose it. The coalition publishes *Censorship News* five times a year, articles, various reports, and background papers. Papers include "Censorship's Tools Du Jour: V-Chips, TV Ratings, PICS, and Internet Filters."

National Coalition for the Protection of Children & Families
800 Compton Rd., Suite 9224, Cincinnati, OH 45231-9964
(513) 521-6227
fax: (513) 521-6337
Web site: www.nationalcoalition.org

The coalition is an organization of business, religious, and civic leaders who work to eliminate pornography. It encourages citizens to support the enforcement of obscenity laws and to close down neighborhood pornography outlets. Publications include the books *Final Report of the Attorney General's Commission on Pornography*, *The Mind Polluters*, and *Pornography: A Human Tragedy*.

People for the American Way (PFAW)
2000 M St. NW, Suite 400, Washington, DC 20036
(202) 467-4999
fax: (202) 293-2672
e-mail: pfaw@pfaw.org
Web site: www.pfaw.org

PFAW works to promote citizen participation in democracy and safeguard the principles of the U.S. Constitution, including the right to free speech. It publishes a variety of fact sheets, articles, and position statements on its Web site and distributes the e-mail newsletter *Freedom to Learn Online*.

FOR FURTHER READING

Books

Randall P. Bezanson, *How Free Can the Press Be?* Urbana: University of Illinois Press, 2003. Explores the changes in understanding of press freedom in America by discussing nine of the most pivotal and provocative First Amendment cases in U.S. judicial history.

Elaine Cassel, *The War on Civil Liberties: How Bush and Ashcroft Have Dismantled the Bill of Rights.* Westport, CT: Lawrence Hill, 2004. Examines the foundations of the war on terror and investigates the loss of the civil liberties of American citizens and legal immigrants.

David B. Cohen and John W. Wells, eds., *American National Security and Civil Liberties in an Era of Terrorism.* New York: Palgrave Macmillan, 2004. A collection of essays examining whether the United States can maintain its dedication to protecting civil liberties without compromising security.

David Cole, James X. Dempsey, and Carole Goldberg, *Terrorism and the Constitution: Sacrificing Civil Liberties in the Name of National Security.* New York: New Press, 2005. Dempsey, former assistant counsel to the U.S. House Judiciary Subcommittee on Civil and Constitutional Rights, and Cole, a law professor and leading civil liberties lawyer, provide an analysis of the constitutional costs of the war on terrorism.

Katherine B. Darmer, Robert M. Baird, and Stuart E. Rosenbaum, *Civil Liberties vs. National Security in a Post 9/11 World.* Amherst, NY: Prometheus, 2004. A discussion by leading experts, on the trade-offs between national security and civil liberties.

Alan Dershowitz, *Shouting Fire: Civil Liberties in a Turbulent Age.* Boston: Little, Brown, 2002. A civil liberties expert discusses how censorship, torture, and curtailment of civil liberties by the government may sometimes be necessary.

Mike Godwin, *Cyber Rights: Defending Free Speech in the Digital Age.* Cambridge, MA: MIT Press, 2003. A discussion of civil liberties in relation to the Internet, including some of the major historical cases involving constitutional rights and the Internet.

Marjorie Heins, *Not in Front of the Children: "Indecency," Censorship, and the Innocence of Youth*. New York: Hill & Wang, 2002. The author suggests that children do not need to be protected from indecent material through censorship.

James Ronald Kennedy, *Reclaiming Liberty*. Gretna, LA: Pelican, 2005. An examination of the way civil liberties in the United States have eroded over the past hundred years, and suggestions on how to reclaim them.

Nan Levinson, *Outspoken: Free Speech Stories*. Berkeley: University of California Press, 2003. This collection contains the stories of twenty people who refused to let anyone whittle away at their right to speak, think, create, or demur as they pleased.

Aryeh Neier, *Taking Liberties*. New York: Public Affairs, 2005. The founder and director of Human Rights Watch—the world's leading rights watchdog organization—examines the history of human rights and civil liberties.

Eric D. Nuzum, *Parental Advisory: Music Censorship in America*. New York: Perennial, 2001. Offers a complete chronicle of the music that has been challenged or suppressed—by the people or the government—in the United States.

Diane Ravitch, *The Language Police: How Pressure Groups Restrict What Students Learn*. New York: Knopf, 2003. A discussion of how textbooks for youth have been censored by schools and publishers.

Mark Sidel, *More Secure, Less Free? Antiterrorism Policy and Civil Liberties After September 11*. Ann Arbor: University of Michigan Press, 2004. Offers a comprehensive analysis of the full range of antiterror initiatives undertaken in the United States after the 2001 terrorist attacks.

Harold J. Sullivan, *Civil Rights and Liberties: Provocative Questions & Evolving Answers*. Upper Saddle River, NJ: Prentice-Hall, 2005. A collection of questions about civil liberties in the United States followed by essays that answer each question.

John Ziegler, *The Death of Free Speech: How Our Broken National Dialogue Has Killed the Truth and Divided America*. Nashville, TN: Cumberland House, 2005. Discusses the effect the news media have had on censorship in the United States.

Periodicals

Bob Barr, "Patriot Fixes," *Wall Street Journal,* November 12, 2004.

Peter Berkowitz, "Two Out of Three Ain't Bad," *Weekly Standard,* July 19, 2004.

Joseph Bottum, "The Library Lie," *Weekly Standard,* January 26, 2004.

Stephen Chapman, "Indecent Moves Toward Federal Censorship," *Conservative Chronicle,* February 25, 2004.

Erwin Chemerinsky, "Giving Up Our Rights for Little Gain," *Los Angeles Times,* September 27, 2001.

David Cole, "Outlaws on Torture," *Nation,* June 28, 2004.

Mark Engler, "Homeland Security for Whom?" *Z Magazine,* September 2003.

Amitai Etzioni, "Better Safe than Sorry," *Weekly Standard,* July 21, 2003.

Nat Hentoff, "War on the Bill of Rights," *In These Times,* September 29, 2003.

Michael Ignatieff, "Lesser Evils," *New York Times Magazine,* May 2, 2004.

Gary Indiana, "Kiss Your Rights Goodbye," *Village Voice,* August 25–31, 2004.

Issues & Controversies On File, "Broadcast Decency Rules," April 30, 2004.

Pramila Jayapal, "Speaking for Justice," *Yes!,* Winter 2003.

Kenneth Jost, "Civil Liberties Debates: Are Rights Being Lost in the War on Terrorism?" *CQ Researcher,* October 24, 2003.

E.V. Kontorovich, "Make Them Talk," *Wall Street Journal,* June 18, 2002.

Stephen Lubert, "Toward Purposeful Dissent," *American Legion,* June 2004.

Thomas F. Powers, "When to Hold 'Em," *Legal Affairs,* September/October 2004.

Kristie Reilly, "Warning: You Are Being Watched," *In These Times,* October 13, 2003.

Kenneth Roth, "In Bush's America, Rules of War Trump Civil Law," *Los Angeles Times,* January 4, 2004.

Alexander Solzhenitsyn, "Live Not by Lies," *Index on Censorship,* February 2004.

Jonathan Turley, "Liberty Ebbs by Degrees," *Liberal Opinion Week*, January 13, 2003.

Patricia Williams, "To See or Not to See," *Nation*, June 28, 2004.

Kathy Young, "Under the Radar," *Reason*, July 2004.

Web Resources

Center for Democracy and Technology (www.cdt.org). Offers civil liberties news and events, educational material, and links to civil liberties–related sites.

Families Against Internet Censorship (www.netfamilies.org). Offers basic information on civil liberties in relation to the Internet, links to other sites, and daily news on Internet free speech issues.

First Amendment Center (www.firstamendmentcenter.org). This Web site features comprehensive research coverage of key First Amendment issues and topics, a First Amendment Library, and guest analyses by legal specialists.

Focus on the Family (www.family.org). Contains numerous articles advocating restriction of media content for the protection of children.

Free Expression Policy Project (www.fepproject.org). Provides research and advocacy on free speech, copyright, and media democracy issues, as well as links to other resources.

Parents Television Council (www.parentstv.org). A grassroots effort to prevent violence and profanity in entertainment, this site offers fact sheets, publications, reference materials, and links.

Project Censored (www.projectcensored.org). This Web site tracks the news published in independent journals and newsletters, and compiles a list of the stories that have been censored by the major news media.

INDEX

Czolgosz, Leon, 75

Jam Master Jay (Jason Mizell), 72
Japanese Americans, internment of, 63, 78

Kaiser Family Foundation, 37
Khawly, Carol F., 98

Levine, Judith, 33
libraries
    should use Internet filters, 41–42, 44–45
        con, 47–49, 51
    technology subsidies to, 50
Library Services and Technology Act (1996), 41
Lincoln, Abraham, 57, 71
Lindh, John Walker, 80
Locke, John, 91
Lockhart Commission, 36–37
London, Herbert, 67

Madison, James, 92
Mapplethorpe, Robert, 119
McKinley, William, assassination of, 75–76
McVeigh, Timothy, 78
Meese, Edwin, 38
Meese Commission, 37
Mineta, Norman, 68
Minow, Newton, 32
Mizell, Jason (Jam Master Jay), 72
Money, John, 37

Moore, Sara Jane, 78
Moustapha, Sidina Ould, 11
MTV (Music Television), 30, 37
Muhammad, John, 76

Nairobi, U.S. embassy bombing in, 108–109
National Endowment for the Arts, 119
National Security Entry-Exit Registration System (NSEERS), 101
New York Society for the Prevention of Cruelty to Children, 35

O'Connor, Sandra Day, 13
Odeh, Mohamed Sadeek, 108–109
Oklahoma City bombing (1995), 78
ordered liberty, 91–92

Padilla, José, 9–10, 80
Parents Television Council, 39
Parker, Jim, 75
Patriot Act (2001)
    civil liberties are threatened by, 84–87
        con, 96–97
    oversight of, 95–96
    provisions of, 92–93
    public support for, 92

PICTURE CREDITS

Cover: AP/Wide World Photos

Daniel Acker/Bloomberg News/Landov, 93, 114

AFP/Getty Images, 28

AP/Wide World Photos, 10, 14, 43, 116

Adam Berry/Bloomberg News/Landov, 55

© Bettmann/CORBIS, 64, 79

Mike Blake/Reuters/Landov, 35

Dennis Brack/Bloomberg News/Landov, 31

Laura Cavanaugh/UPI/Landov, 72

© Jacques M. Chenet/CORBIS, 23

Rebecca Cook/Reuters/Landov, 86

© CORBIS SYGMA, 108 (both)

Larry Downing/Reuters/Landov, 96

© Najilah Feanny/CORBIS, 47, 50

Getty Images, 25, 82, 94, 100, 102, 103

Erik S. Lesser/Getty Images, 48

Library of Congress, 62

© Wally McNamee/CORBIS, 36

Ethan Miller/Reuters/Landov, 120

© Michael Newman/Photo Edit, 44

Sue Ogrocki/Reuters/Landov, 80

Paramount/The Kobal Collection, 121

© Mark Peterson/CORBIS, 70

Photos.com, 17

Spencer Platt/Getty Images, 56

Reuters/Dave Ellis/POOL/Landov, 76

© Shaul Schwarz/CORBIS, 85

© Mike Simons/CORBIS, 12

Mario Tama/Getty Images, 52

Mike Theiler/Landov, 69

Time Life Pictures/Getty Images, 19, 38

Victor Habbick Visions, 18, 30, 110, 115

Jim Watson/U.S. Navy, 107

Tim Wimborne/Reuters/Landov, 58

ABOUT THE EDITOR

Andrea C. Nakaya, a native of New Zealand, holds a BA in English and an MA in communication from San Diego State University. She has spent more than three years at Greenhaven Press, where she works as a full-time book editor. Andrea currently lives in Encinitas, California, with her husband Jamie. In her free time she enjoys traveling, reading, gardening, waterskiing, and snowboarding.